The

Game

Of

God

Carol —
Thanks for the support.
Enjoy The Game!
Arthur B. Hancock
Kathleen J. Brugger

THE GAME OF GOD

Recovering Your True Identity

ARTHUR B. HANCOCK
KATHLEEN J. BRUGGER
CARTOONS BY ARTHUR B. HANCOCK

HUMANS ANONYMOUS PRESS

Humans Anonymous Press,

P.O. Box 170045, St. Louis MO 63117.

ISBN: 0-9634203-0-5

Library of Congress Catalog Card Number: 92-73760

Cover Design by Rebecca Lowers

Special thanks to Jean Brugger for her love,
support, and partnership.

CONTENTS

To You

Allons! whoever you are come travel with me!

Travelling with me you find what never tires.

The earth never tires,

The earth is rude, silent, incomprehensible at first, Nature
  is rude and incomprehensible at first,

Be not discouraged, keep on, there are divine
  things well envelop'd,

I swear to you there are divine things more beautiful than
  words can tell.

—Walt Whitman, Song of the Open Road

INTRODUCTION

WHY WE NEED TO FORGIVE GOD

"And don't tell me that God moves in mysterious ways," Yossarian continued, hurtling on over her objection. "There's nothing so mysterious about it. He's not working at all. He's playing. Or else He's forgotten all about us. That's the kind of God you people talk about—a country bumpkin, a clumsy, bungling, brainless, conceited, uncouth hayseed. Good God, how much reverence can you have for a Supreme Being who finds it necessary to include such phenomena as phlegm and tooth decay in His divine system of creation? What in the world was running through that warped, evil, scatological mind of His when He robbed old people of the power to control their bowel movements? Why in the world did He ever create pain?"

—Joseph Heller, Catch-22

A friend recently told us that,

  of all the funerals he had ever attended,

    he had yet to hear a minister

      satisfactorily answer

        the question,

          "Why did God create death?"

He went on to say that,

  in fact, he had yet to hear

    a minister (priest, rabbi, etc.)

      make any sense of why God had created

        anything at all.

Our friend concluded that

  the most sensible explanation

    for this dangerous and mysterious universe

      is simply that **there is no God**.

We live on a tiny planet

  lost in a huge and seemingly indifferent universe.

    Life is a continuous struggle

      which inevitably ends with death.

        LIFE IS A TERMINAL DISEASE.

What kind of universe is this anyway?

Does life have any meaning or purpose?

If there is a "God," why did God create the universe?

Many religions

have tried to explain

God's motives for creating the universe—

a universe filled with suffering and death—

but these theologies are often

illogical and filled with contradictions,

and thus fail to provide comfort

when a **true** test arises:

when real disaster strikes.

A minister once told us that, in his experience,

the death of a child was particularly

difficult to "explain,"

and often resulted in

expressions of

hatred for God

by the parents,

and even the abandonment

of their faith.

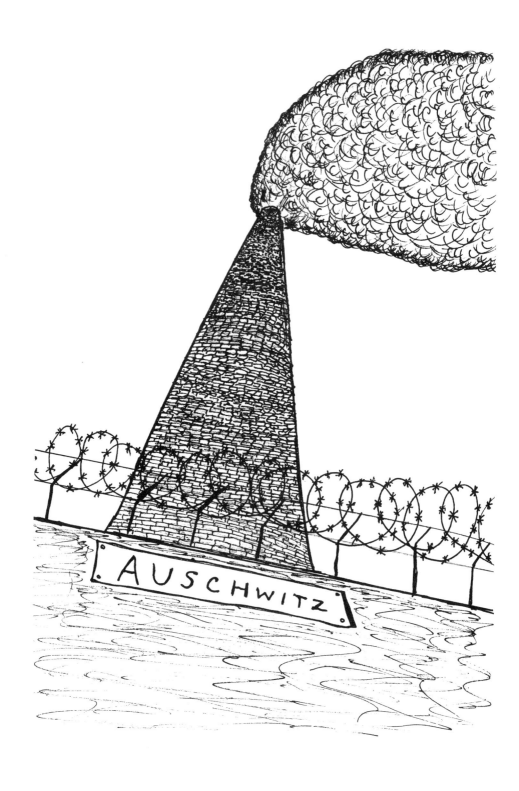

Whatever "His-Her-Its" motives,
  (let us not sex-type the Creator!)
how could a "loving" God
knowingly create a universe
which is capable of **this** kind of cruelty:

death,

concentration camps,

torture,

child molesting,

murder,

rape,

war,

disease,

mental illness,

starvation,

greed,

addiction,

violence,

racism,

gossip,

sexism,

etc., etc., etc.?

The child's question,
"Why did God let my puppy die?",
cannot be satisfactorily answered by
most of the theologies
of the world.

We are told
we must "love" the Creator,
but **how can we**
when we behold
His-Her-Its creation—
a creation which lacks
any sensible explanation
for suffering, ignorance, and death?

It might be argued
that the "positive" aspects of life
are reason enough to love God,
but the question remains:
Can all the good in the world
justify the suffering
of a single one of God's creatures?

JUDGMENT DAY
East and West

It would seem that the best we could do
would be to fear our Creator,
and to suppress our anger towards a Supreme Being
Who **chooses** to remain silent and aloof
while humanity writhes in ceaseless agony.

Some religions believe
that the ultimate horror comes **after** life—
to those who, after a brief lifetime
in a world of total confusion,
fail to locate and "correctly" believe in God.
These "sinners," "infidels," etc.,
wind up in a place of
never-ending torture, called "hell."

Other religions believe
in an endless cycle of birth and rebirth—
that unless we live an exemplary life,
we are doomed to return to
the hellish struggle for "another round."

Both theologies appear to have one thing in common:
**wretched humanity is held hostage
by the whim of God.**

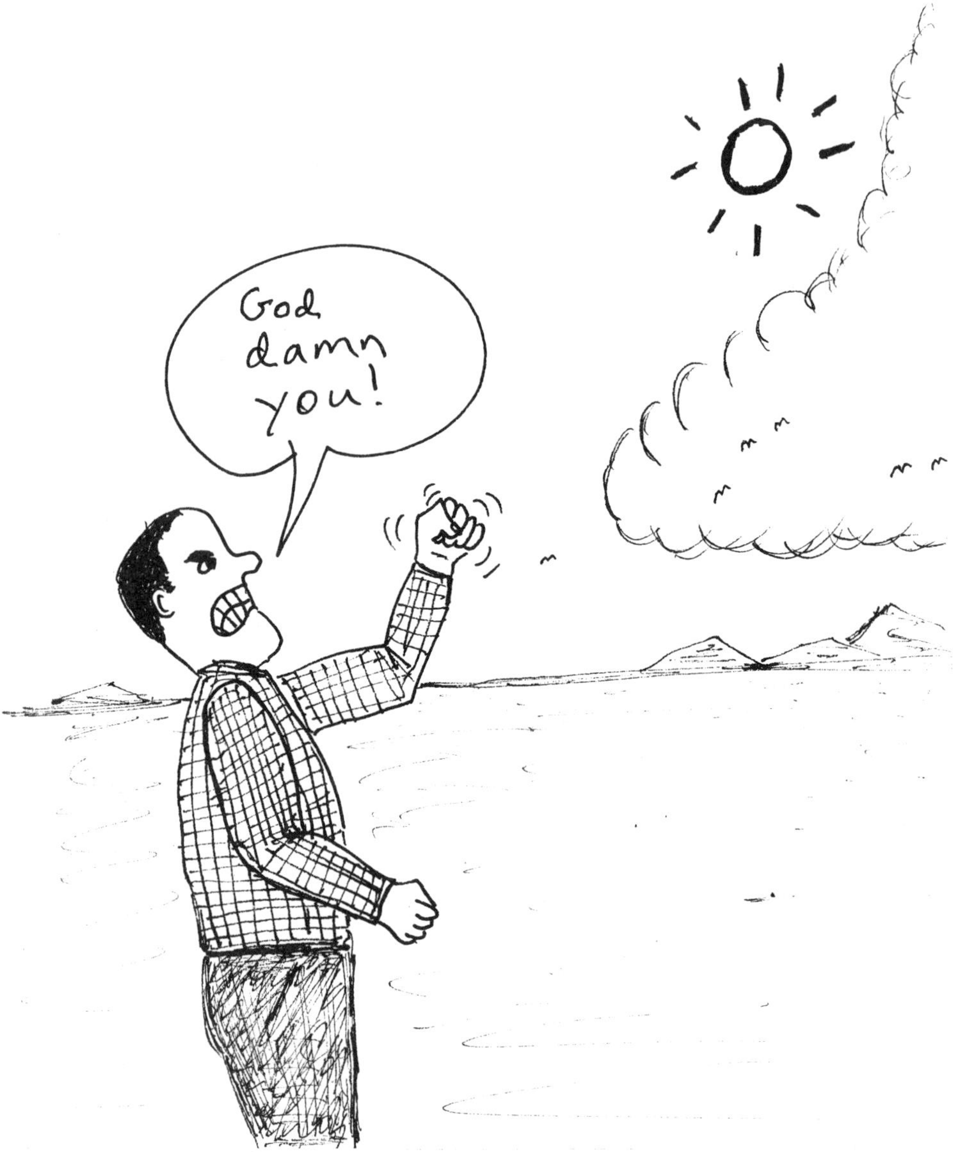
God damn you!

Saints throughout the ages have declared:

WE MUST LOVE GOD,
and the only way we can know we are
loving God is when we are
loving all of creation.

The loveless state of the world shows that "love of God" is, to put it mildly, exceedingly rare. There is a reason for this: there is something **blocking** our love for God. This "something" could only be **fear**, thus **anger**, towards God.

The basis of all fear is the unknown.
The basis of all hatred is fear.
What we fear is what we hate.
What we hate is what we fear.

We are afraid of a mysterious God
Who would make a universe of suffering,
and we are angry at this God
for putting US in it!

We cannot love God until we can forgive God.

THE DAILY GLOBE

Vol. 150, Number 28   anyday

Mass Murderer Stalks City

latest victim

HAITI HAS H-BOMB

New superpower Lists Demands

Water revealed to cause Cancer

"We've Had it Folks," say top experts

ozone

Day Care Center Was running "Dial-a-child" prostitution ring

Woman Shoots Dog, Then Self

THE GAME OF GOD

As long as we see the Creator as **separate** from creation, as many do, we can only be resentful towards the Creator (no matter how deeply we deny and suppress it), because

She-He-It must have

KNOWINGLY

created suffering in others

(THIS MEANS US).

An all-powerful Creator Who deliberately creates suffering in inferior creatures is a monster. The notion of "free will" (self-inflicted suffering) is ludicrous because God, as creator of **all**, must have **created evil** in order to give us a "choice"! Observably, God created humans with an overwhelming inclination to "choose" evil (count the true saints). Therefore, to be punished by God, for succumbing to the tempting evil She-He-It *created*, is unfair, to say the least!

It is quite impossible to fear and hate God and love God at the same time.

We fear and hate God because we are misunderstanding God's nature.

Until we face the existence of our fear and anger towards God, and relinquish it by gaining a deeper understanding of God, we can **never love God.**

THE LOGICAL SCIENTIFIC VIEW:

The entire universe suddenly spewed out of absolutely nothing, and many billions of years later, rocks turned to meat and started thinking.

THE ILLOGICAL METAPHYSICAL VIEW:

The universe was created deliberately by something we do not yet understand, for purposes we are only beginning to fathom.

This book is about recovery in the ultimate sense of the word: in the sense of *universal recovery*. What most of us think of as the *evolving* universe will be presented as the *recovering* universe. What the universe is recovering is consciousness that was **intentionally** lost. What the universe is recovering *from* is the pain that is the **intentional** result of **intentionally** lost consciousness.

We will present the theory that paradise was **intentionally** lost—for the pleasure of regaining it. The universe was created as a Game...for the experience of hell and for the experience of recovering heaven.

Without Intentionality, that is, without a deliberate Creator, the universe is devoid of all purpose and meaning. In a Godless universe the life of a saint and the life of a hired murderer would be equally "worthy" and equally pointless. We hold that an intentionless universe is the stuff of madness. Sanity demands a Purpose. Intentionality requires a Conscious Creator.

We will offer a theoretical model of Creator and creation as **ONE**. The universe, we will assert, is a Game of God. We hold that this model allows us to absolutely forgive, and thus absolutely love, God.

Loving God is the only way to win the Game.

PART ONE

THE INCENTIVE TO PLAY

I want to know how God created this world. I am not interested in this or that phenomenon, in the spectrum of this or that element. I want to know God's thoughts, the rest are details.

—Albert Einstein

I cannot believe that God plays dice with the cosmos.

—Albert Einstein

1

THE PROBLEM WITH HAVING IT ALL

Under heaven all can see beauty as beauty only because there is ugliness.
All can know good as good only because there is evil.

Therefore having and not having arise together.
Difficult and easy compliment each other.
Long and short contrast each other;
High and low rest upon each other;
Voice and sound harmonize each other;
Front and back follow one another.

—Lao Tsu, Tao te Ching

INFINITY

Why would God create the Universe?

In order to attempt to answer this essential question

we need to first try and imagine who God is.

The word *God* is surely the most misunderstood—

thus abused—word in any language.

For the sake of our argument,

let us agree on this definition of "God":

the conscious creator of the universe.

We will use the word "God" throughout this book.

While it seems presumptuous folly to attempt

to understand God from our ant-like perspective,

the truth is that we are all attempting it anyway

(believer and non-believer alike).

Therefore,

let us consider the following **theory**

and see how well it holds up logically.

"In the beginning" was God.

God is absolute awareness.

God is the absolute awareness of absolute reality.

God is eternal and all-knowing.

God has no limits.

God is absolutely unlimited.

THE BANK of WILDEST DREAMS   today
"we aim to please."
                              $ 1,000,000,000,000,000,000.

        PAY TO: (your name here)
THE SUM OF: ONE BILLION TRILLION DOLLARS

For: Anything You Like!
                                        OFFICIAL SCRAWL

What does having no limits look like?

As all of us are limited this is very difficult to visualize, but let's try anyway.

Let us attempt to make *you*, for example, as unlimited as we can.

To get things rolling, let's imagine that you have one billion trillion dollars.

At an interest rate of 5% per year, you would have an income of nearly one million trillion dollars a week without touching the principal...let us guarantee that you would always be this rich.

Now let's make you
  the most physically beautiful,
    intelligent,
      talented,
        happy person on Earth.

We'll also give you
  total love for everyone and everything,
    complete satisfaction,
      and eternal life in perfect health.

You never make a mistake,
you are never afraid or in doubt.

You have complete power,
you are made King or Queen of the Earth.

You are at perfect peace,
you love everyone and everyone loves you.

In short,
you have no problems whatsoever.

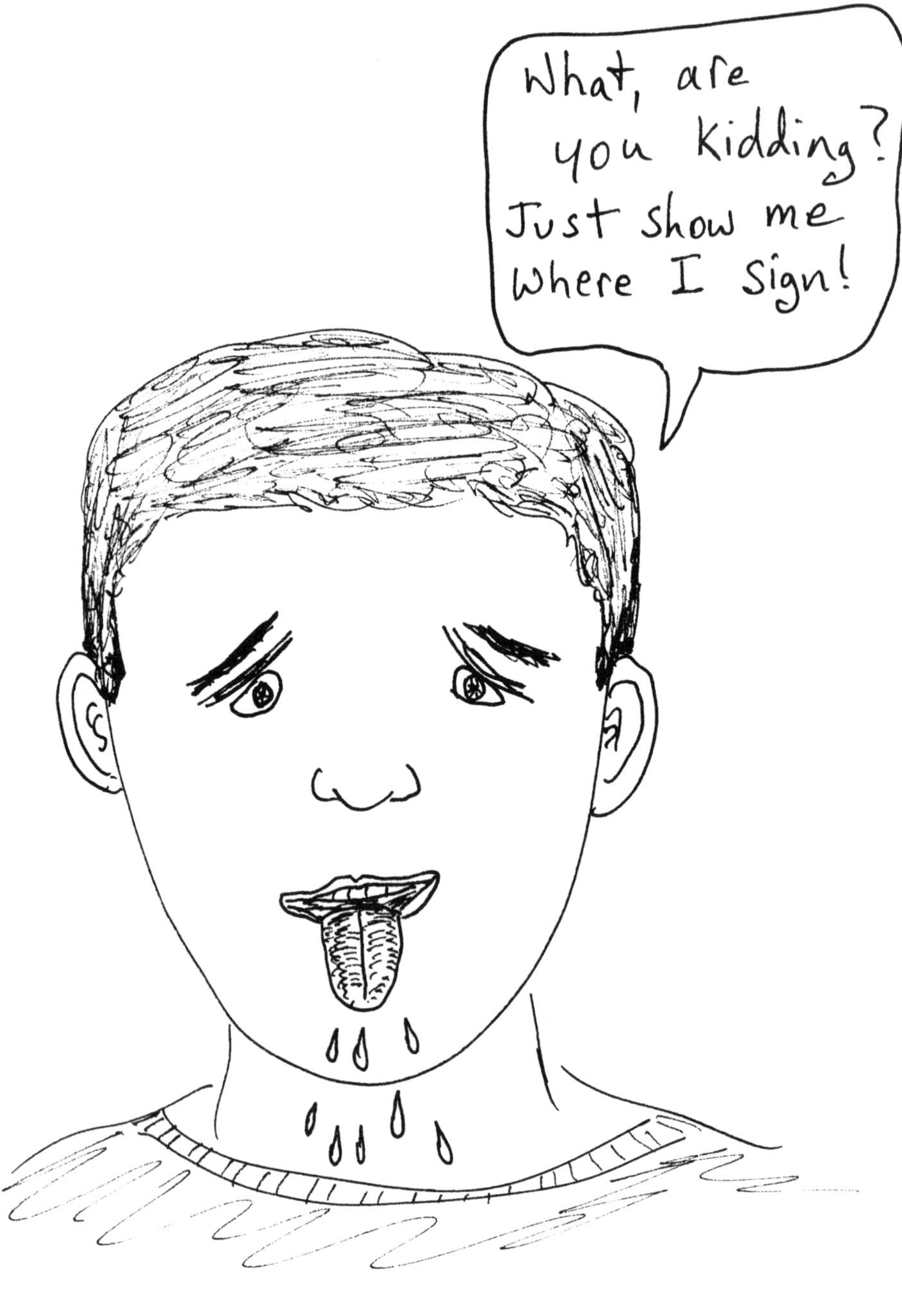
What, are you kidding? Just show me where I sign!

Sounds good, right?

As illogical as this might sound, can you see any

limitations to being unlimited?

Any limitations to being:
all-knowing,
immortal,
wealthy,
healthy,
loving,
satisfied,
wise,
and
problem-free?

Let's look.

BIKE WORLD

Remember a time

when you

really

wanted

something

...but couldn't afford it.

Remember
    how you **saved** your money to buy this
        desired thing,
    how you **anticipated** ownership,
    how you spent countless hours **dreaming**
        about it,
    how **happy** you thought you would be when
        the day finally arrived when you would
        own it?

As a sextillionaire, it would soon be **absolutely impossible** for you to experience **anticipation** or **longing** for anything with a price tag. Price could literally never be an object.

What's wrong with this?" you might ask.

There's nothing "wrong" with it—in and of itself—we are merely pointing out a "limitation" to being incredibly wealthy: **the inability to experience poverty and deprivation.**

It is

    an interesting

        and observable truth

            that

                anticipation

            is often more pleasurable than

                possession.

(The object of one's desire, once attained, can often become commonplace and routine.)

Therefore,

    to be denied

        the experience of

            anticipation

                is no small thing.

Might there be some other experiences denied to you, the "person who has it all"?

How about the **inability to fall in love?**

"But," you might say, *"I thought you said I was already in love with everyone?"*

Exactly.

Because you **are** in love with everyone, it is impossible for you to ever experience **falling** in love (suddenly shifting from a loveless state into the experience of love).

Another interesting and observable truth is that

the experience of falling in love

is made precious,

like a diamond,

due to its

rarity.

Again, to be

denied the experience

of this ecstatic shift,

from lovelessness to love,

is no small limitation.

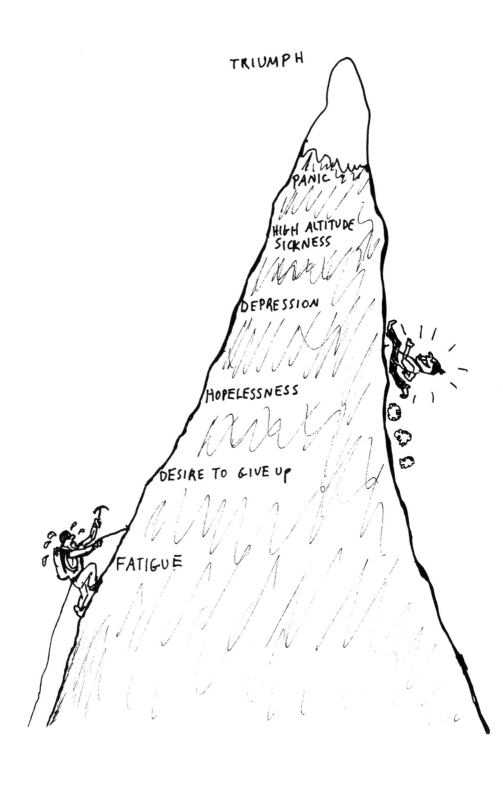

Let us see if we can detect other limitations that are

the inevitable consequence

of "having it all."

If you never make a mistake

and never have a problem,

it is impossible for you

to ever have the experience of **defeat**,

or the experience of **struggle**

required to overcome an obstacle,

or the experience of **triumph**

when the obstacle is overcome.

This process:

the risking of defeat, the struggle against it,

the sting of failure, or the triumph of success,

virtually defines life as we know it,

and to be denied

the experience of this process

is no small thing.

EEEEEEEEEEEEEEEEEEEEEE

THE SCREAMING DEATH'S HEAD

World's
MOST
Terrifying
Attraction!
the
Screaming
Death's
Head!

Finally (though we could easily go on), your state of immortality would make it impossible for you to experience that perpetual fear of death which haunts all living things...as well as the experience of death itself.

"Surely," you might say, *"there could be nothing negative about this!"*

Let's see. With your survival assured, you could never be afraid of **anything**, you would have nothing to lose, there would not be the slightest tension or risk in all of life.

You would be like a person who "gambled" for eternity and could not lose: who won every game every time. "Winning" would lose all meaning, as "life" without death would lose all meaning.

Death is the ultimate unknown and
being denied the experience of fearing it
(the unknown is the source of all fear),
as well as the very experience of death,
is, again, no small thing.

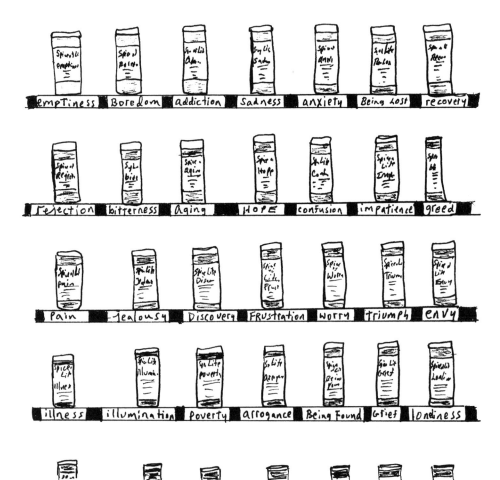

THE SPICE OF LIFE SELECTION

emptiness | Boredom | addiction | Sadness | anxiety | Being Lost | recovery

rejection | bitterness | Aging | HOPE | confusion | impatience | greed

Pain | Jealousy | Discovery | Frustration | worry | triumph | envy

illness | illumination | Poverty | arrogance | Being Found | Grief | loneliness

Looking, then, at "having it all," we see that you do **not** really "have it all" after all—that any number of very high-quality experiences are utterly denied to you.

But again you might ask, *"Why bother with all of these* **negative** *categories?"*

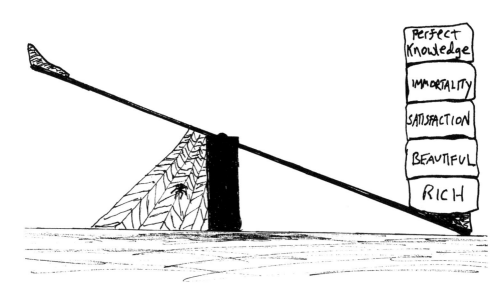

These "negatives" are the obstacles which make the experience of life interesting. A life comprised of all "positives" would be a life without challenge...there would be no growth because there would be no incentive to grow. There would be no need to change because **everything would be fine exactly the way it is.**

But would it really be "fine"?
Experiences on the "negative"
(adventurous and exciting?)
part of the scale would be
FOREVER DENIED
you.

Should you ever wish to experience any "negatives" you would be unable to do so...in fact **you could never even have the wish!**

YOU WOULD BE STUCK AS "YOU" FOREVER!

After a few million years or so of being healthy, wealthy, and wise, can you see that there might be a certain nightmarish **sameness** to "having it all"?

FIFTY BILLION
YEARS LATER...

We know someone who

as a small child

used to have a horror

not of hell,

but of heaven.

He would sit

and think

about never-ending "eternal life"

and slowly begin

to chant the word

    forever, and

        forever, and

            forever...

until he would be almost

frozen in

terror

at the idea of

ceaseless

existence

in some **static** location—

no matter how glorious—

and **no way out!**

IGNORANCE
DEATH
dissatisfaction
UGLY
POOR
Perfect Knowledge
IMMORTALITY
satisfaction
Beautiful
RICH

A fine balance

of positives and negatives,

of weaknesses and strengths,

of wisdom and foolishness,

of laughter and tears,

of love and hate,

of life and death,

is what makes for

growth

and action

and purpose

and meaning...

and the possibility of

a way out of SAMENESS!

2

THE LIMITATION
OF THE UNLIMITED

"Once upon a time, I, Chaung-tzu, dreamt I was a butterfly, flittering hither and thither, to all intents and purposes a butterfly...suddenly I awoke...Now I do not know whether I was then a man dreaming I was a butterfly, or whether I am now a butterfly dreaming I am a man."

—Chaung-Tzu

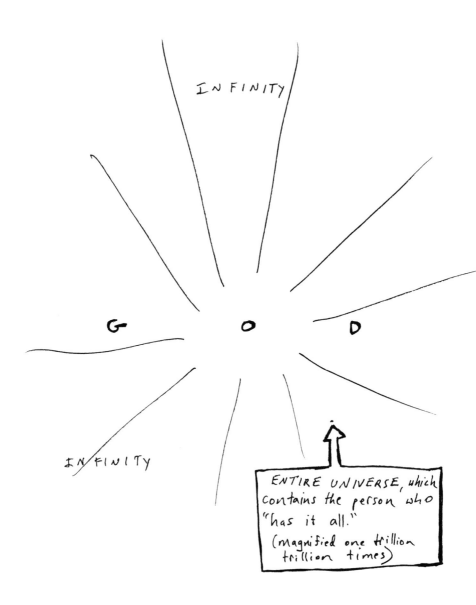

Let's get back to God, and the question:

WHY WOULD GOD MAKE THE UNIVERSE?

God, as opposed to our person who "has it all" (but really doesn't), is, according to our definition, *truly* unlimited.

Surely God "has it all"!

God is **absolutely unlimited.**

The person who "has it all," for example, is still just one person who is limited to a single point of view, while

God is INFINITE AWARENESS.

If the experience of limitation is denied to the person who "has it all," how much more must the experience of limitation be denied to the Creator?

Let us remember our model of God as
   eternal,
    all-powerful, and
    all-knowing.
God is the absolute awareness of everything.
    Nothing is hidden from God.
   All is known to God.
   Nothing is stronger than God.
Therefore, there can obviously be no experience of
   limitation possible to God.
God, as supreme awareness, is absolutely
   unlimited.

But

if no experience of limitation is possible to God,
THEN GOD IS LIMITED AFTER ALL!

The "inability"

of unlimited God

to experience limitation

IS a limitation—and thus a contradiction.

In order for God to be **absolutely** unlimited,

God **must** be able to experience limitation.

BUT HOW?

How could God have a quality (realistic) experience of limitation, while being absolutely unlimited at the same time?

This is in keeping with the riddle:

Can God create a boulder too heavy for God to lift?

Because God is truly unlimited,

there is only the illusion of contradiction...

God has "solved the problem."

We shall soon see how...

The question will arise, *"Why in the universe would the Creator wish to experience limitation?"*

The answer is certainly not "because God is bored." Boredom is a state of limitation and God is absolutely unlimited.

Our answer is that *God has a playful nature.*

The incentive to play can be found in the words of British mountain climber George Leigh Mallory, when asked why he wished to challenge the icy heights of Mt. Everest:

BECAUSE IT'S THERE.

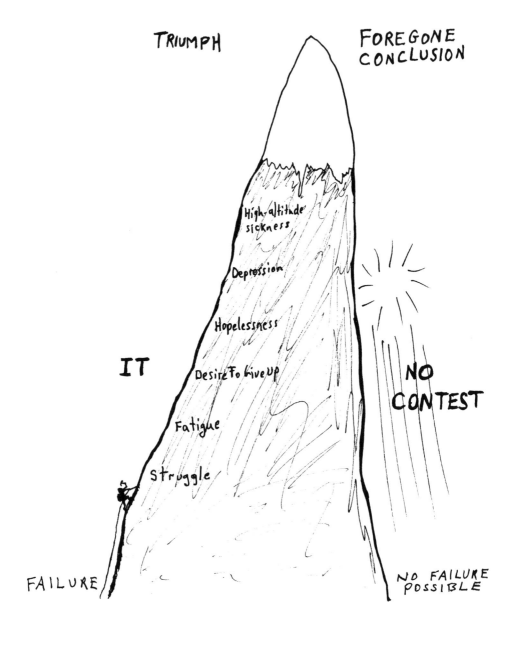

What did George Mallory mean,

"*because it's there*"?

Because the mountain is there,

therefore one must climb it?

No, Mallory meant

because **IT** is there—

"it" being

the struggle, the challenge,

the obstacle, the risk,

the definition of self, the potential for triumph:

over the climber's limitation,

and over the limitation imposed by ice and rock.

This, and more,

is the "it" that is there.

God

cannot experience

"IT"

as conscious God.

There is an old song about a millionaire who liked to go slumming. He dressed in rags, rode the rails, hung out in cheap bars, and picked up old floozies.

When recognized and asked why he behaved like this, he replied (in the chorus):

"After you've been eating steak a long time,

beans, beans taste fine!"

Let's say that God wanted to **experience poverty.**

Even God in the

poorest rags

would still be

conscious God,

and therefore

could not possibly

have the experience

of what it is to be poor

(the fear...

the desperation...

the hopelessness...).

There would not be

the slightest

experience of

quality

limitation.

Some religions teach that
God has created a universe of limitation
and observes it from a detached perspective.

This would be like looking at fish in an aquarium—
one has the experience of **observing** fish,
but not of **experiencing** fish.

Thus an external or separate God
has the experience of **observing** limitation,
but not of **experiencing** limitation.

This cannot be the solution to our question:
How can the unlimited experience limitation?

THE PROBLEM:

CHOOSE **ONE:**

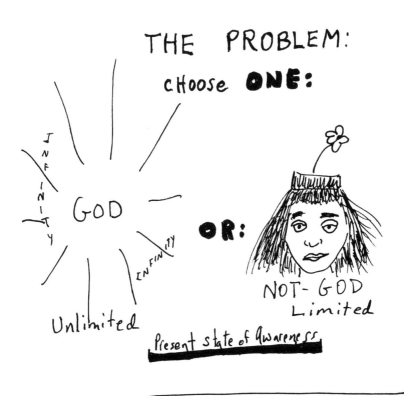

GOD

INFINITY

INFINITY

Unlimited

OR:

NOT-GOD
Limited

Present state of awareness

THE SOLUTION:

Who the hell am I?

INFINITY

INFINITY

Present state of awareness

There is logically only

ONE WAY

in which God could have the experience of limitation.

GOD MUST,

FOR THE DURATION

OF THE EXPERIENCE

OF LIMITATION,

FORGET THAT SHE-HE-IT

IS GOD.

Recall our millionaire who enjoyed a bean diet every now and again. Just as he could never forget that help was only a phone call away (which greatly diminished his "experience of poverty"), so then God, penniless and in rags, could *instantly* get out of any "tight spot" (which thus could never even be experienced as "tight").

Let us envision another scenario. What if the millionaire's chauffeur, before depositing his ragged master on skid row, administered a powerful drug which would utterly block the master's memory.

Lost in amnesia,

abandoned in rags,

without identification,

and thus unable to call upon his vast resources,

the rich man would have

a quality experience of limitation indeed.

The solution, then,

to the "inability" of the unlimited to experience limitation,

is **self-induced amnesia.**

THE UNIVERSE IS GOD

IN A SELF-INDUCED STATE OF AMNESIA.

PART TWO

GAME IN
PROGRESS

I consider that our present sufferings are not worth comparing with the glory that will be revealed in us. The creation waits in eager expectation for the children of God to be revealed. For the creation was subjected to frustration, not by its own choice, but by the will of the one who subjected it, in hope that the creation itself will be liberated from its bondage to decay and brought into the glorious freedom of the children of God.

—Paul, Romans 8:18-21

3

THE
REUNIFICATION
OF HUMPTY

The joy, the triumph, the delight, the madness!
The boundless, overflowing, bursting gladness,
The vapourous exultation not to be confined!
  Ha! ha! the animations of delight
  Which wraps me, like an atmosphere of light,
And bears me as a cloud is borne by its own wind.
                          —*Percy Bysshe Shelly, Prometheus Unbound*

...this most beautiful system of the sun, planets, and comets,
could only proceed from the counsel and dominion of an
intelligent and powerful Being.
                          —*Isaac Newton*

UNIVERSE!
a game o' God
never-ending amusement!
Allows

1. G.O.D.___ to experience NOT-God

2. not-God to experience God
   and

3. God to experience not-God

Our *amnesia theory* asserts that God created the
   universe in order to experience limitation, and
   achieved this experience via self-induced amnesia.
We hold that God **chose** to have this experience
   because it was His-Her-Its *pleasure* to do so.
Any activity undertaken strictly for pleasure must be
   considered an amusement.
We hold that God created a universe of limitation in
   order to play in it.

The universe is a God-class game.

What would be the purpose of this game?

We maintain that there are three purposes:
   1. **For the unlimited to experience limitation.**
   2. **For the limited to experience the unlimited.**
   3. **For the unlimited to experience the unlimited.**

The universe is a game in which God forgets
   His-Her-Its identity, and, in the process of playing,
remembers Who She-He-It is.

The Universe
less than one second old
(ACTUAL SIZE)

The next few chapters will examine the First Purpose:
for the unlimited to experience limitation.

While no one knows how God did it,
let's say that God created the amnesia/universe
through the creation event
which scientists call the Big Bang
(we will use the Big Bang model
whether or not it ultimately proves to be correct).

Let us imagine that,
at the moment of creation,
God-consciousness
e   x   p   l   o   d   e   d
into innumerable separate forms of
unconsciousness.

Following the Creation Event,

    every "particle" that

        "came into existence" would be

            identical

in one essential way:

    every particle would be God in amnesia.

God-awareness,

    a supreme Oneness

        now *apparently* shattered into innumerable pieces,

 would

    amnesiacally identify with,

        and behave as,

            whatever particle it happened

to be momentarily "trapped" *as.*

Remember that this is all an *amnesiac illusion*...

    God is always whole and One.

        Even if Jill has amnesia and imagines she is Jack,

            she is still Jill.

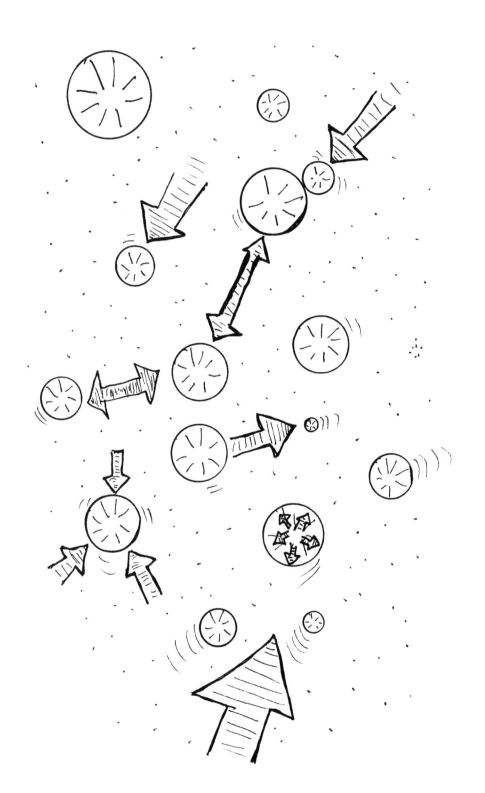

Initially the universe would be completely unconscious: as far from God-awareness as it is possible to get. This would be desirable in order to totally obliterate all memory and sense of identity: a highly effective method by which God covered His-Her-Its tracks! This would make for a convincing illusion of limitation.

"In the beginning" (less than one second after the big bang), elementary particles were created, and began to be passively arranged, by the four interactional forces.

These forces,
    gravity,
      electromagnetism,
        the strong nuclear force, and
          the weak nuclear force,
are actually the creative will of God—
the dynamic creators and destroyers of matter.

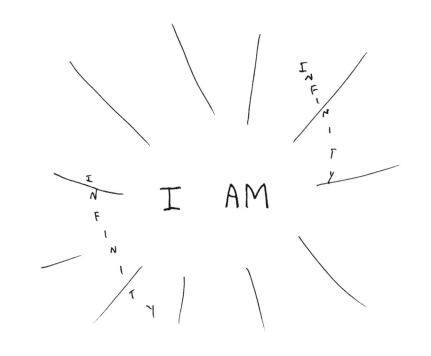

BEFORE

AFTER

We hold that there are three universal laws.

We will discuss the first two laws now,

and the third later.

The First Law of the Universe is:

EXIST AS FORM.

Until God created a universe of forms,

there was only God,

Who is infinitely One.

Anything *infinite* is without boundary or limitation,

and, therefore, cannot be considered a "form" or "thing."

A form is any thing defined by a boundary

which delineates it from something "else."

There is, in truth, nothing "else" than God.

There is only the deliberate illusion of "something else."

The Second Law of the Universe is:

SURVIVE AS FORM.

Until God created a universe of survival,

there was only God,

Who is eternal.

Infinite Oneness can never be anything other

than Infinite Oneness,

therefore it can never change,

it is immutable,

it can never die.

The concept of "survival" only exists

in the deliberate illusion of form/duality.

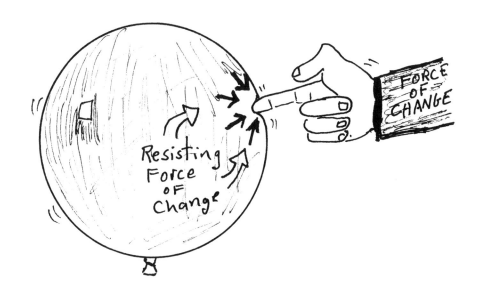

Balloon attempting
to maintain its existent
structural integrity.

What does **survival** *mean?*

When a form is attempting to survive,
   what is it doing?

We think it is trying,
   to the best of its ability,
      to "hold itself together" through time.

We define survival as:
   the effort of a specific form to maintain
   its existent structural integrity.

In other words,
   survival is the energy expended by a form
      for its self-preservation.

If forms did not attempt to survive, there would be no process of growth, accretion of matter, or increase in form complexity (particles would not even form, thus no visible, ordered universe could evolve).

The elementary particles began to draw together and form atoms (communities of particles). These communities were formed because the interactional forces, the will of God, dictated that there be a universe of visible forms.

When a particle becomes a part of an atom, it abandons what we will call its

primary survival identity,

called "particle," and identifies (becomes one) with the larger form. Now, instead of a primary survival identity called "particle," we have a primary survival identity called "atom."

We will define primary survival identity as:

the essential structure of a form

which dictates its survival behavior.

This definition applies to all particles and communities of particles (every form) in the universe. An electron can only behave/survive like an electron, an elephant can only behave/survive like an elephant, and so on.

CHANGE

PAST
Existent
Structural
Integrity

PRESENT
Existent
Structural
Integrity

Note
alteration
of structure.
The "past"
form will
never be
duplicated.

Time | 1 microsecond   2 microseconds

The failure of a
particular form to
maintain itself unchanged
through time.

Evolution

is the historical process of

s t r u g g l e

between the forces of change and the

attempt of forms to remain unchanged.

An extremely important observation

is that while all forms **attempt**

to maintain their existent structural integrity through time,

this effort is actually **FUTILE**.

No physical form survives unchanged

from one instant to the next.

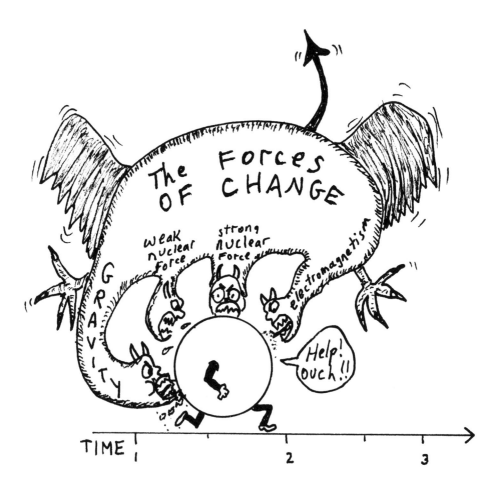

If you could be frozen at the temperature of absolute zero,

 just as you are this instant,

  with every subatomic particle

   preserved motionless in place,

  you would have accomplished form-survival's goal

 of perfectly maintained structural integrity through time.

As it is, the instant that all of the

 trillions of particles that comprise you have

  shifted, changed, disappeared, or been added to

 (which happens across every two

  consecutive measurable units of time),

 the "old" you of an instant before is *gone forever.*

The "old you" has literally **died**

 as that particular structural configuration:

  a configuration which can never be duplicated again.

Every physical form in the universe

 (from atom to humpback whale) is

  failing to maintain itself unchanged through time...

   every physical form in the universe

   is "dying" constantly.

  THE SURVIVAL EFFORT EQUATES
  CHANGE WITH DEATH.

We have stated that God's First Purpose
in creating the universe
was to experience limitation.
God never intended, however,
to remain in the state of limitation *forever*
(this state is only part of the fun)!
The Second Purpose is about
returning to God-consciousness.

The evolution of the universe
is literally the process of
God-in-amnesia reawakening into God-identity.

The universe could be seen as
Humpty Dumpty,
who took a great fall.
Survival-based evolution could be seen as
all the king's horses and all the king's men
trying to put Humpty together again
(that is, efforting to re-establish
Humpty's original structural integrity)...
working to bring order out of chaos.

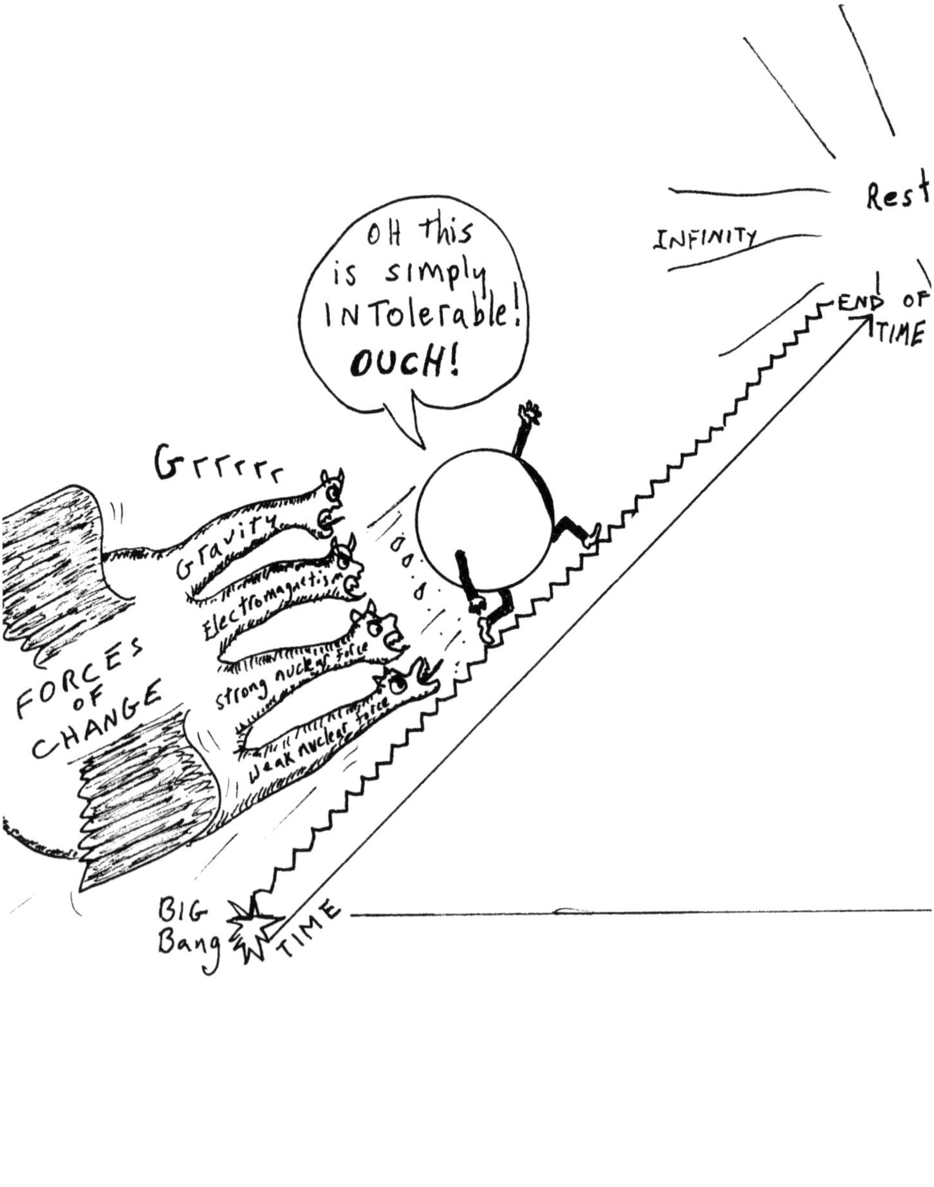
OH this is simply INTolerable! OUCH!
Grrrrr
Rest
INFINITY
END OF TIME
FORCES OF CHANGE
Gravity
Electromagnetism
strong nuclear force
weak nuclear force
BIG Bang
TIME

Evolution is driven or motivated entirely by survival.

Evolution seeks "rest" from change and death
through the establishment of
perfect changeless order
throughout the universe...
that is, the complete reunification of Humpty.

There is no "place of rest"
in form's perpetually failing attempt
to maintain itself unchanged through time.
Change (interpreted as death) haunts all form,
and becomes increasingly painful and frightening
as form becomes aware.

Evolution
is driven by
the intolerable nature
of chaos and failed survival effort.

The motivation for evolution is fear of death.
Existence as form is intolerable
because survival as form is impossible.

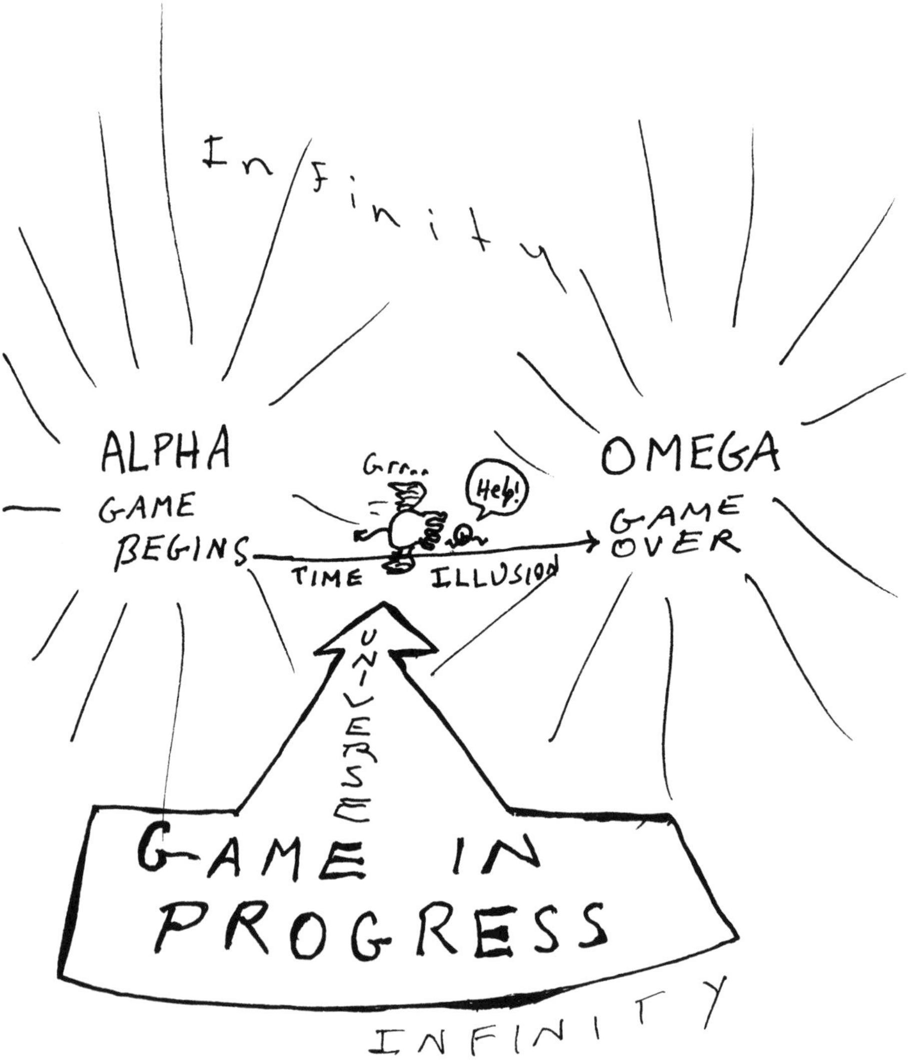
Infinity
ALPHA
GAME BEGINS
Grrr..
Help!
OMEGA
GAME OVER
TIME
ILLUSION
UNIVERSE
GAME IN PROGRESS
INFINITY

The Universe Game

(The Reunification Of Humpty)

is a process of going

from complete unconsciousness

(death and separation)

to a fully awakened consciousness

(eternal oneness).

4

EVOLUTION OF
THE GAME

We now believe with confidence, that the whole of reality is one gigantic process of evolution. This produces increased novelty and variety, and ever higher types of organization; in a few spots it has produced life; and, in a few of those spots of life, it has produced mind and consciousness.

—*Sir Julian Huxley*

This secret spoke Life herself unto me: "Behold," said she, "I am that which must ever surpass itself."

—*Nietzsche*

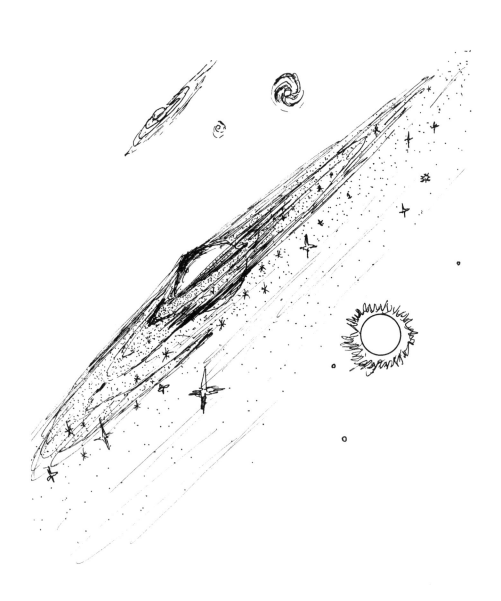

Let us look at the unfolding of the Universe Game more closely. We will use generally accepted scientific theory and will see how well it supports the amnesia theory.

In the Big Bang, the universe exploded into being.
God-as-form had come into being.

God, Who is infinite
(infinite *includes* every thing but *is* no thing),
had "become" some thing.

For a long time the universe was filled only with inorganic forms (elementary particles, atoms, and molecules) which were passively manipulated and arranged by the interactional forces.

We call these forms **"non-volitional"** because of their inability to react to their environment. These forms are acted *upon* by the environment.

Non-volitional forms are the building blocks of
galaxies,
stars, and
planets.

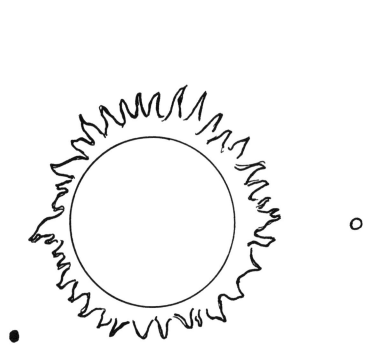

When a certain

second or third-generation

star is born

(containing the heavy elements essential to life

which were produced by an earlier star),

and when this star

has a planet

in an orbital zone conducive to life,

the stage is set

for the introduction of

volitional forms,

or "life."

KA ZAAM!

GREAT MOMENTS IN EVOLUTION:
the dawn of life

Billions of years ago,

on the planet we call Earth,

when all of the required conditions were perfect,

a chemical reaction was triggered

and unicellular life forms were created in the sea.

This was the most

significant advance

in planetary evolution

since Earth's creation.

God-as-form had become ALIVE!

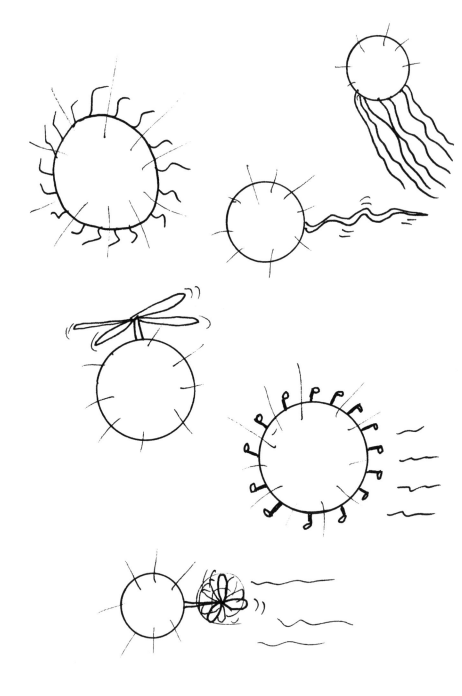

Locomotion

Necessity is the Mother of Invention

For the first time,

forms were not merely

manipulated

by the interactional forces,

they now possessed

rudimentary **choice**

about how they would react

to their environment.

Eventually,

forms developed methods

of propelling themselves

and thus became even more self-determined.

God-as-form could move!

EARLY LIFE-FORMS
IN
Relationship

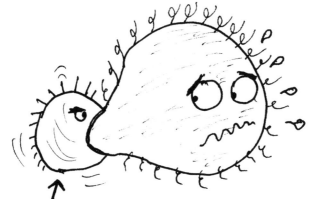

SMALLER BUT
HUNGRIER

The same forces,

gravity, electromagnetism,

and the strong and weak nuclear forces,

which brought these volitional forms

into existence,

were still operating

as the organizing principle of life.

In fact,

the "choices"

that the volitional forms now had

were nothing more than an evolved expression

of these basic underlying forces.

This means that the natural law:

superior force always overcomes weaker force

continued unabated in the realm of life.

The design of all living things

(from the shape of a fish

to the color of a bluebird's beak)

is determined by the **interaction of forces.**

The behavior of all living things

(from a virus to a violinist)

is determined by the **interaction of forces.**

mammals
(200 million)

Land vertebrates
(325 million)

insects
(375 million)

?

Life migrates to Land
(400 million)

Vertebrates
(500 million)

Crustaceans
(600 million)

Flatworms + Jelly fish
(700 million years)

Alright!

Sex
(800 million years ago)

Plants
(1.5 billion years ago)

KA-ZAAM!

Living Cells / VOLITIONAL UNIVERSE
(3.5 billion years ago)

TIME

Big Bang

NON-VOLITIONAL UNIVERSE

Remember that evolution is about
  putting Humpty together again.

The process of bringing order from chaos
  (consciousness from unconsciousness)
demands the development of
  ever-increasingly complex forms.
As forms evolve, they become larger and more complex and
  appear to survive more effectively (superficially, forms
seem to survive unchanged through longer spans of time
  when actually they are changing/dying constantly).
Increased form complexity and the *illusion* of prolonged
  survival are, we shall see, necessary in order to achieve
an essential future goal of the Game: self-awareness.

In the world of cell-eat-cell,
  the name of the game
is optimal survival.

Evolution is the same throughout the universe—
  a form evolves/changes **only** to enhance its survival
(no form would have come into
  existence had it been otherwise).

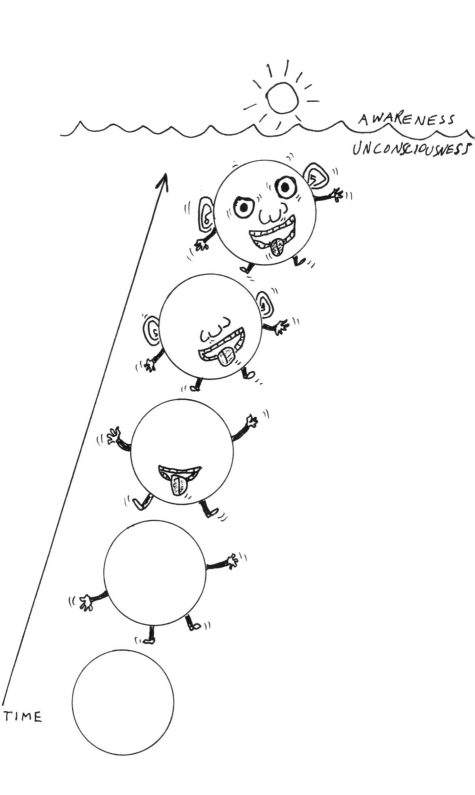

Forms became more complex:

Forms developed nerve sensors...

and **God-as-form could feel**.

Forms developed tongues...

and **God-as-form could taste.**

Forms developed noses...

and **God-as-form could smell**.

Forms developed ears...

and **God-as-form could hear**.

Forms developed eyes...

and **God-as-form could see**.

What is occurring

is the evolutionary process of

God-as-form slowly becoming aware

("*The better to feel/taste/smell/hear/see*

you with, my dear.")

from a totally unconscious state of amnesia.

INCORRECT MODEL

CORRECT MODEL

God experiencing form

God is not sitting inside a form being God.

God is in a self-induced state of amnesia,
and is totally identifying
with form.

All volitional forms
(plants and animals)
are attempting to survive in the same way:
through **flight/fight survival behavior.**

When confronted by the forces of change,
volitional forms can only
flee from (flight) or aggress against (fight)
the threat to their existent structural integrity.

THE ONLY CHOICES AVAILABLE TO A SURVIVING LIFE-FORM ARE FLIGHT OR FIGHT.

(There is, however, an alternative to surviving as a life-form, which we will discuss later.)

Once again,
flight/fight behavior is simply
the evolved expression
of the primal forces.

Life is arranged through the interaction of forces;
a balance of powers.

Let us visualize the planet Earth,

    now teeming with life forms,

as the "Garden of Eden"—

    a place of unquestioned obedience to natural law.

From the smallest one-celled organism

    to the most complex animal,

no form in this pristine environment was capable of

    questioning or challenging

the rules of the Game.

    The Garden of Eden

    has often been thought of as

    paradise.

    In truth,

    the "garden" was a balance of raw power:

    an unconscious state of

    eat-or-be-eaten, kill-or-be-killed;

    a place of ruthless and unceasing survival behavior.

    The Garden of Eden, while magnificent,

    was completely under the spell of amnesia.

God may have chosen the experience of amnesia

but God did not intend to remain in it forever.

God intends to awaken.

HUMPTY WAS BY NO MEANS COMPLETE.

God-as-form was alive.

God-as-form could move.

God-as-form could feel.

God-as-form could reproduce.

God-as-form could taste and smell.

God-as-form could hear and speak.

God-as-form could see.

God-as-form could even remember a bit.

But one thing God-as-form could not yet do.

Without this critical function

the second purpose of the Game

(*the limited experiencing the unlimited*)

could never be realized.

GOD-AS-FORM COULD NOT INVENT PURE NONSENSE.

It was time for the next major step

in evolution to occur.

The stage was set for human beings.

5

THE HUMAN BEING

Sitting under the stars in Africa, on the Serengeti plains, I am a tiny and insignificant speck, less vital to the life around me than the hyena I hear calling. She, after all, is an intrinsic part of this eternal cycle of life and death. My thirty years of work with chimpanzees has taught me humility: we humans are not, after all, separated from the rest of the animal kingdom by an unbridgeable chasm. The hyena, like the chimpanzee, can think and reason. There is continuity in the evolution of mind as well as of physical structure.

—*Jane Goodall*

The dawn of humankind was the most significant event in evolution since the creation of life forms. Evolution had produced a creature who was destined to become **self-aware** (a very essential step in the Game, as we shall see).

What separated Homo sapiens from the rest of the natural order?

The separation was accomplished via the ability to engage in analytical thought and to form abstract conclusions—

    beginning with ideas like

        "tools" and

          "fire-keeping"

        and evolving to concepts like

          "good" and

           "evil."

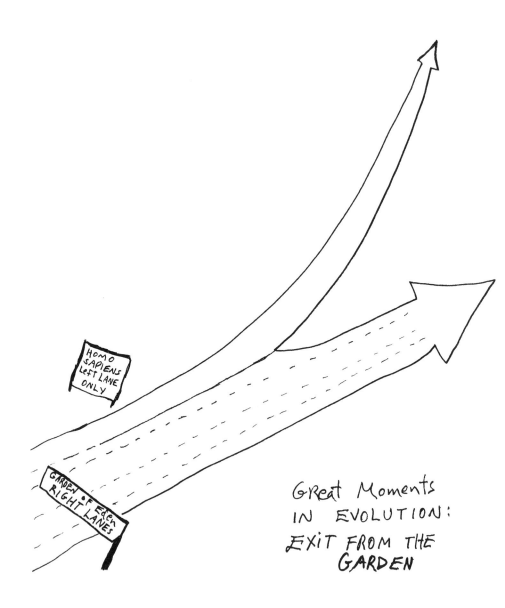

HOMO SAPIENS LEFT LANE ONLY

GARDEN OF EDEN RIGHT LANES

Great Moments
IN EVOLUTION:
Exit FROM THE
GARDEN

While the development

　　of abstract thought

　　　　was a continuation

of orderly evolution,

it nonetheless

　　required

　　　　a **departure**

from the "Garden"

of mindless

obedience.

To see an example of that process which separated humanity from the "Garden," let's examine the evolution of an abstract thought—an **idea**.

Let us say that a prehistoric woman named Oogah stands at the bank of a river she cannot cross, gazing longingly at a bunch of bananas on the other side.

Oogah remembers times when she has crossed rivers on fallen trees. She then notices that the tree next to her is leaning across the river.

As stored memory data and

the present environmental input

merge,

an **idea** forms in Oogah's mind.

She "sees something" in the physical reality before her that does not yet exist:

if she could make the leaning tree fall,

she could cross the river on its back.

Oogah has just invented the bridge.

Even though natural bridges have always existed, what Oogah has invented is

a CONCEPT of *bridge.*

Oogah tells the tribe of her idea,
  it is tested (or she is burned at the stake),
    it is found to work,
      and a measure of control
        over the river (and nature)
        has been attained.

Human civilization has evolved
  from precisely such concepts.

These original abstractions
  initiated the departure of humanity
    from unquestioned obedience
      to physical reality
        (before Oogah,
          when a river blocked the way,
            there was nothing to be done).

Past

Memory: crossing
River on Fallen tree

Memory: seeing
tree fall

Memory: seeing
leaning object
fall flat

PRESENT

RIVER
BLOCKING Path,
Leaning
Tree,
Bananas
on other
side of
RIVER

IDEA!

PRESENT
EMPTY STOMACH
SIGNALS HUNGER +
GROWING FRUSTRATION

Let's look more closely at how Oogah arrived at her creative idea.

It was

stored memory data

(crossing rivers on trees)

coupled with the

sensory input and survival demands

of the present environment

(leaning tree, sight of bananas, hunger)

which permitted

the necessary **associations** to occur

and to synthesize

into an **idea**.

It was expanded memory storage which permitted the dawn of analytical thought.

To analyze means to "*sift available information*," and memory storage is the essential provider of that information. In order to store sufficient memory for abstract thought, a large and sophisticated brain had to first be evolved.

Memory is utilized, like everything else, only to enhance the survival of the organism. The rudiments of memory-assisted logic can be found in the wild animal kingdom.

Some animals use tools (an ape probing an ant hill with a stick, for example). Animals are capable of learning lessons. For example:

An animal attacked by a tiger at a water hole would probably form no associations (a tiger attack could happen anywhere).

But should the animal be attacked by the tiger
a second time at the same location
it is likely that the animal will *logically conclude* (based on memory records of the first attack) that:

   this particular spot is tiger-infested
   and deserving of extra caution
   or complete avoidance in future.

Animals are only capable
of the most primitive mental associations,
whereas humans,
with their vastly expanded memory storage capacity,
are able to realize far more complex abstractions.

The twice-attacked animal might well reach such a broad
conclusion as:
"*all water holes draw predators therefore
be on guard*,"
however, this conclusion would never go beyond
"*water holes=extra predator danger*."
A human concept such as "*bridge*" is much more abstract
and therefore can become a general **principle**, with a much
wider application.
For instance, "*bridge*" leads from
"*dropping tree across stream*,"
to innovative construction techniques and applications:
aqueducts, archways, and suspension spans,
as well as to the more purely abstract concept of
"*linkage*."

What we need to notice is that the unfolding of the Game has evolved an entirely new form. Evolution has produced expanded memory, which has in turn produced analytical reasoning. Analytical reasoning has produced abstract concepts. The newly evolved form, the abstract concept, we will call a *thought-form*.

All thought-forms have one thing in common: they represent a departure from the universe of physical form...they are **non-physical forms**.

A non-physical thought-form is a specific mind-generated entity: a thought, belief, concept, etc., accepted as true and stored in the mind.

The thought-form may be chemically synthesized and stored in the physical brain/body, but the **content** of the thought-form, the actual *abstraction*, such as "linkage," does not exist in physical form.

Analytical thought opened the door to true creativity:

the ability to visualize possibilities
within an existent reality which are not
presently manifested.

Once a non-physical form
(a concept, idea, thought, etc.)
is created,
it becomes as real and powerful
in the life of its host as
physical reality
itself.

In fact,
the thought-form and physical reality
become indistinguishable:
our thoughts *become* physical reality.

For example,
even if the twice-attacked animal
never sees the tiger again,
that animal will always approach
that particular water hole
AS THOUGH THE TIGER
WERE THERE.

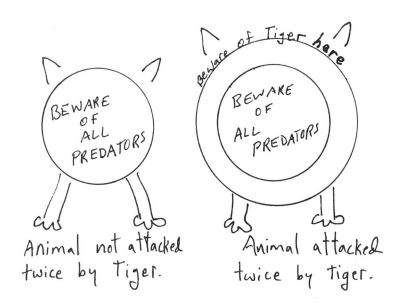

Animal not attacked twice by Tiger.

Animal attacked twice by tiger.

TWO ANIMALS APPROACHING THE SAME WATER HOLE

A thought-form is a specific form which,

considering itself to exist,

is bound by our proposed

Second Law of the Universe

to SURVIVE AS FORM—that is,

to attempt to remain unaltered through time.

This does not mean that this type of

non-physical form is any more "conscious"

of itself than an elementary particle,

it simply means that a specific thought—

beware of tiger here—

has individual existence in itself,

and survives accordingly.

(Each thought-form must be distinct from every other

thought-form or mental chaos would result.)

The emergence of

the non-physical surviving thought-form

was the key to the evolution of human beings.

Another word for the

non-physical surviving thought-form is

belief.

It was by entering into the realm of belief

that humanity left the Garden of Eden behind.

6

PREVAILING BELIEFS

A sense of wonder started men philosophizing, in ancient times as well as today. Their wondering is aroused, first, by trivial matters; but they continue on from there to wonder about less mundane matters such as the changes of the moon, sun, and stars, and the beginnings of the universe. What is the result of this wonderment, this puzzlement? An awesome feeling of ignorance. Men began to philosophize, therefore, to escape ignorance.

—Aristotle

Who can forget Jacob Bronowski, in his superb TV series "The Ascent of Man," standing among the ashes of his relatives at the Auschwitz crematorium and reminding us: "This is how men behave, when they believe they have absolute knowledge."

—Arthur C. Clarke

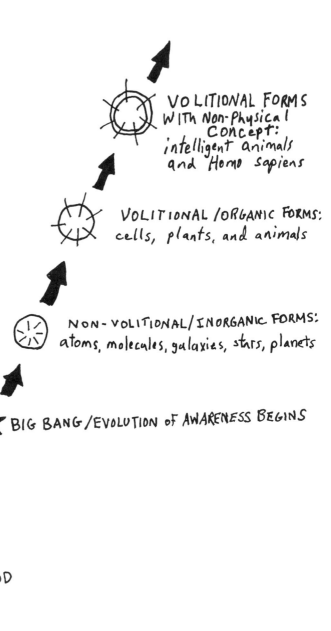

VOLITIONAL FORMS
WITH Non-Physical
Concept:
intelligent animals
and Homo sapiens

VOLITIONAL/ORGANIC FORMS:
cells, plants, and animals

NON-VOLITIONAL/INORGANIC FORMS:
atoms, molecules, galaxies, stars, planets

BIG BANG/EVOLUTION OF AWARENESS BEGINS

GOD

Let's summarize what we have seen of the Game of God thus far.

Unlimited God suppresses His-Her-Its awareness via amnesia and creates a universe of form/limitation.

As evolution proceeds, non-volitional forms become volitional—this is God-consciousness beginning to awaken from deep unconsciousness.

As volitional (life) forms become sufficiently complex, a new level of form is evolved—that of the non-physical realm of belief. This is a further awakening of God-consciousness.

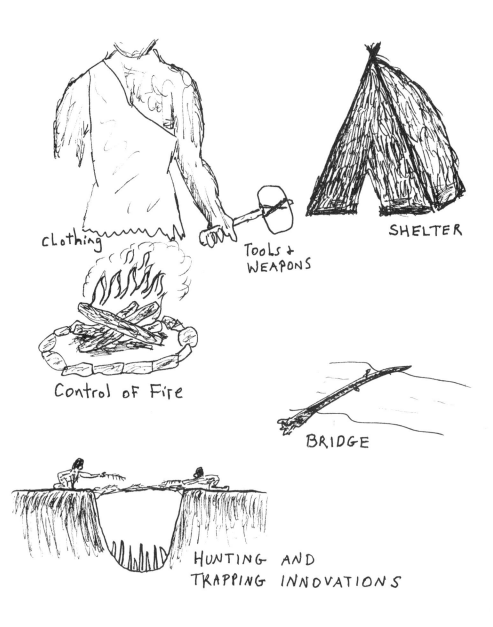

clothing

Tools + WEAPONS

SHELTER

Control of Fire

BRIDGE

HUNTING AND TRAPPING INNOVATIONS

The non-physical thought-forms

we have been looking at so far

(the bridge and the tiger-infested water hole)

are inventions, concepts, associations, conclusions, etc.,

which are strictly concerned with the physical.

The earliest innovative thoughts

were certainly inspired by and focused upon

the physical environment

and the survival needs of the physical body.

We call this category of thought-form

pro-survival fact data.

Anything which can be consistently verified

as true in the physical environment

should be considered a fact.

Facts are always pro-survival

simply because

survival is always enhanced

by accurately perceiving and accepting reality.

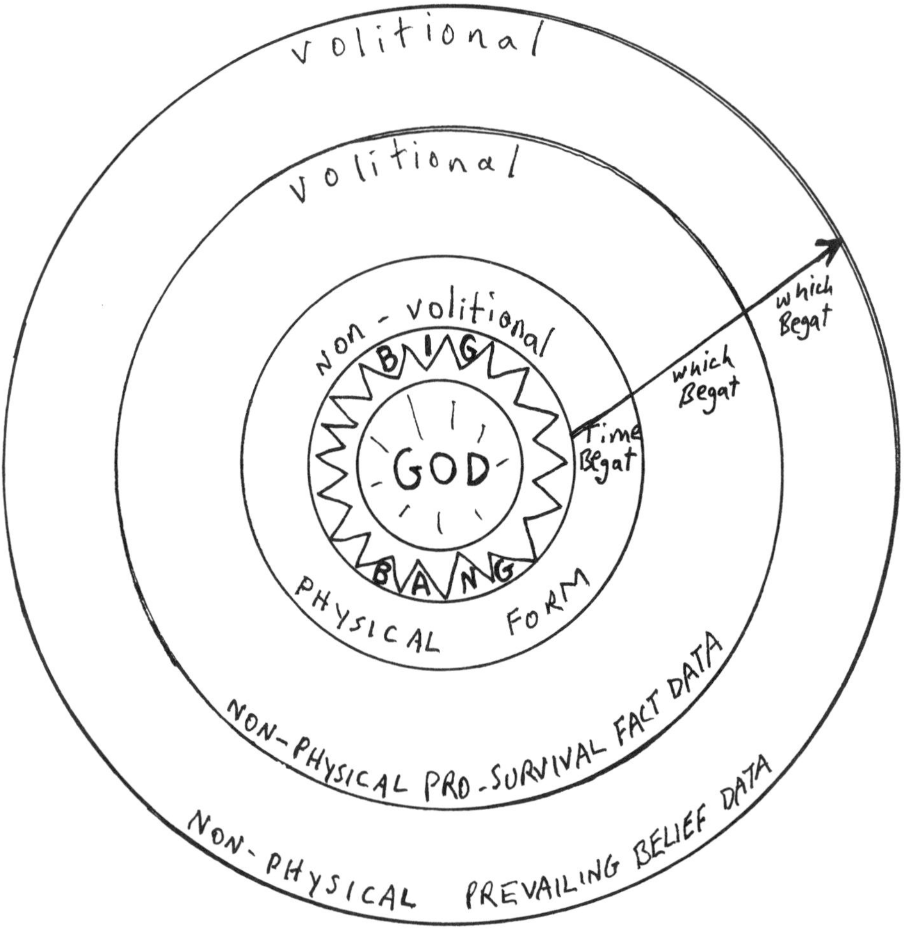
volitional
volitional
non-volitional
BIG
GOD
BANG
PHYSICAL FORM
Time Begat
which Begat
which Begat
NON-PHYSICAL PRO-SURVIVAL FACT DATA
NON-PHYSICAL PREVAILING BELIEF DATA

The true development of humanity as we know it
required the evolution of a vastly more complex non-
physical thought-form.
This category of belief did not require any verification in
physical reality.

Pro-survival fact data was produced by the physical body
interacting with the physical environment.
The mind began as pro-survival fact data, a collection of
thought-forms based upon the logical analysis of the
physical environment (fire is hot, weapons bring food).
As pro-survival fact data accumulated, the mind began to
analyze *it*, and truly abstract thought-forms were born
(the concept of "good" and "evil").
**The new thought-forms were produced by the stored pro-
survival fact data...by the *mind*.**

We call this new thought-form a **prevailing belief**.

Let's look at how prevailing beliefs came to be.

Humans began to view their environment objectively.

Instead of only hunting animals, for example,
our ancestors began painting pictures of them.

This demonstrates an observer point of view,
or subject-object relationship:
　　instead of being *inside* the environment,
　　humans began to look *at* the environment—
　　a perspective which *separated* them from it.

These early cave paintings almost certainly had symbolic
"meaning" of some kind.
　　Even though these paintings depicted
　　　　physical reality
　　　　　　(pro-survival fact data),
　　the **meaning** of the paintings represented
　　　　the realm of non-physical reality; of mind
　　　　　　(prevailing belief).

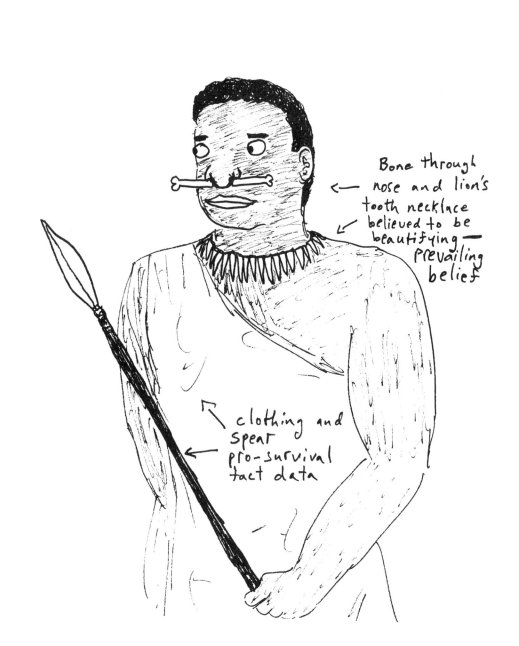

Bone through
nose and lion's
tooth necklace
believed to be
beautifying —
prevailing
belief

clothing and
spear
pro-survival
fact data

Humans were evolved with the power of unlimited creativity.

The power to create means the power to **invent.**

Recall that we have defined "creativity" as the ability to visualize possibilities within an existent reality which are not presently manifested.

(Oogah "visualizing" the tree as a bridge).

"Invent" is defined as:

the act of originating something new.

An important observation is that one can invent either **fact** or **fantasy.**

Thus the same creative ability

which invented the bridge

and the ability to control fire

(pro-survival fact data),

also invented the "spirit" of the hunt

and human "sacrifice" to "appease the Gods"

(prevailing belief data).

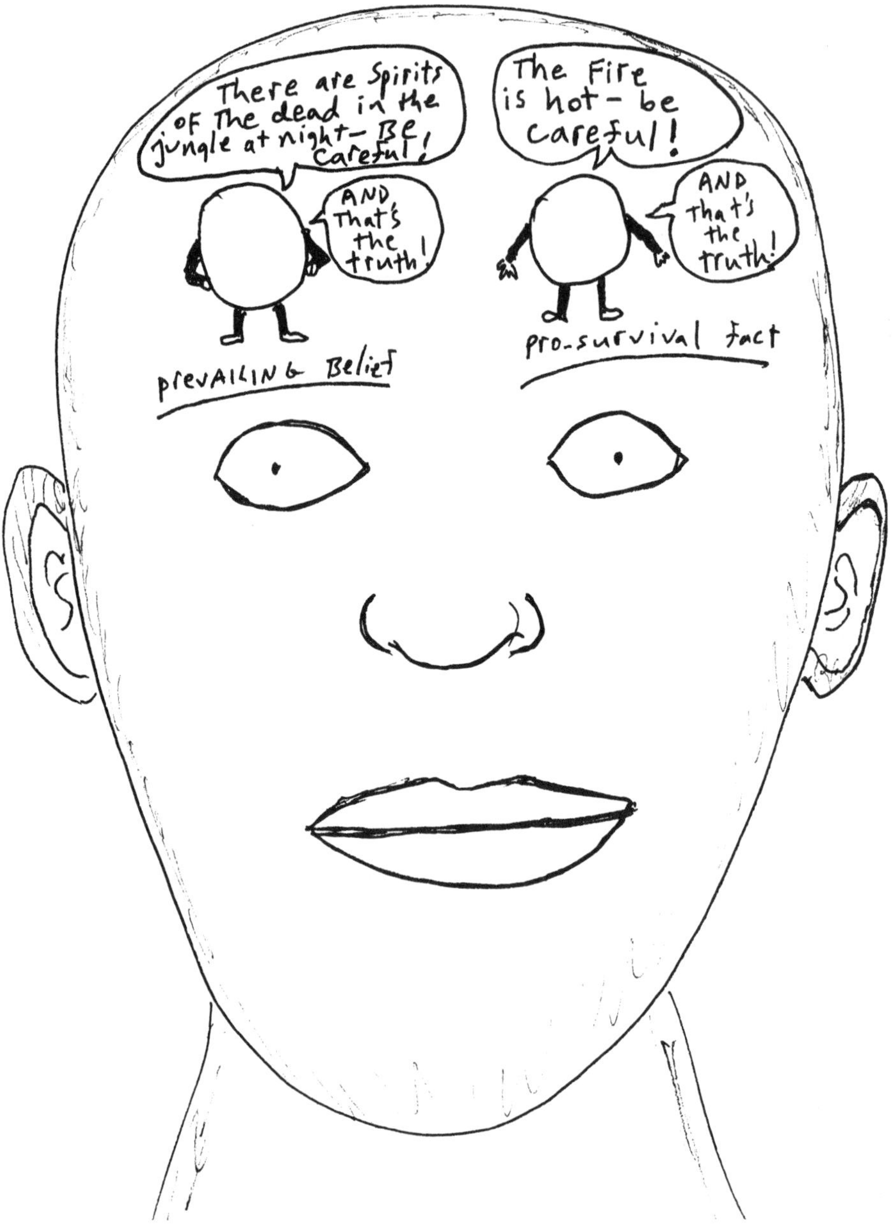
There are Spirits of The dead in the jungle at night– Be careful!
AND That's the truth!
The Fire is hot – be careful!
AND That's the truth!
prevAILING Belief
pro-survival fact

All beliefs, like all experiences, are committed to memory. If this were not the case, we would have to learn everything all over again all of the time.

Two types of information began to fill the human memory banks: pro-survival fact data, and

prevailing belief data.

Both of these categories were stored in the mind as though they were **equally true**.

We define *mind* as: *a memory bank comprised of stored sensory input data, pro-survival fact data, and prevailing belief data.*

The prevailing belief, no matter how unfounded it is in reality, considers itself "to be" and attempts to survive as fully as does the verifiable fact that "*fire is hot*." It cannot do otherwise.

Remember that survival is defined as:

the effort of a specific form to maintain

its existent structural integrity.

A PREVAILING BELIEF MUST ATTEMPT TO MAINTAIN "STRUCTURAL INTEGRITY" AS FULLY AS ANY OTHER FORM (PHYSICAL OR NON-PHYSICAL) IN THE UNIVERSE. WHILE NO PHYSICAL FORM CAN SURVIVE UNCHANGED THROUGH TIME, A NON-PHYSICAL FORM CAN SURVIVE UNCHANGED *FOREVER*.

what is the great light in the sky?
what could it possibly matter? ah, ignorance is bliss!
oh yeah?

A belief must have a believer in order to exist.
A belief can survive unchanged only
by convincing the believer that it is true and
that it is survival-enhancing for the believer.
Prevailing beliefs were inspired
by that which inspires everything in the universe—
SURVIVAL.
As humans became more objectively aware
of their environment,
they became increasingly aware
of their ignorance of it,
and were motivated by survival fears
to attempt to understand it.
To question reality
is to embark into the unknown—
to open a Pandora's box
where answers only lead
to more questions.
The unknown is the source of all fear,
and prevailing beliefs evolved
to combat the unknown
and relieve the fear of it...
a very pro-survival function.

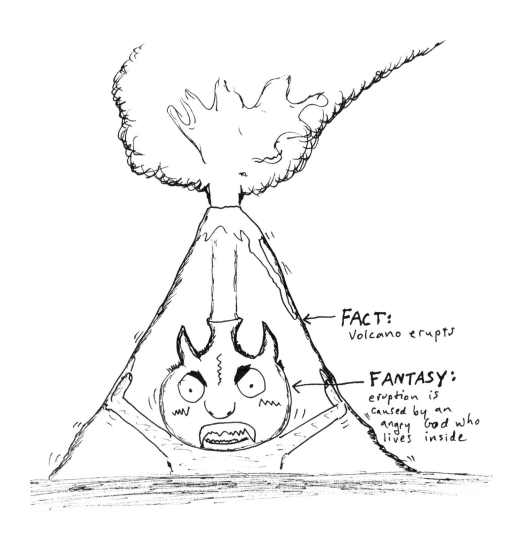

Let's look at the formation of a particular prevailing belief system. Prevailing beliefs "evolve" into more complex structures by "bonding" with other prevailing beliefs.

Let's imagine a prehistoric village which was close to a volcano which erupted occasionally.
The villagers' greatest fear of the volcano
came from **not understanding** this great force:
not knowing the **why** or **when** of an eruption.

The wisest (most inventive) members of the village theorized that an angry God lived within the volcano, and that when this God was disturbed the volcano erupted.
They named the God *Woo* and developed a religion in order to attempt to appease Him.
Woo, as it turned out (as the belief system evolved), had a taste for virgin sacrifices, and this offering was solemnly carried out twice a year.

The religion of Woo provided relief (except for the virgins) from the stark terror of total ignorance and granted the believers a certain degree of comfort within a dangerous and mysterious reality.

Prevailing beliefs misinterpret and manipulate physical reality in order to survive (maintain structural integrity) as "truths."

If the volcano does not erupt,
    this shows that the sacrifice was acceptable
        and Woo is happy.
If the volcano erupts,
    this shows that the sacrifice was not acceptable
                (maybe she wasn't a virgin),
    not that there is no such thing as Woo
                  (blasphemy!).

The doctrine of Woo is fiercely defended because, for the belief, and thus for the believer, it represents life and death survival.

Prevailing beliefs

    are not verifiable in reality and thus

    cannot survive logical examination.

What makes this type of belief so dangerous

is that in order to survive unchanged

it must present itself,

        not as theory limited by ignorance (which it is),

            but as the absolute truth (which it isn't).

The more unprovable a belief,

    the more dangerous it is

    to anyone who disagrees with it.

The greatest threat to a lie is the truth.

People react with hatred when their beliefs are threatened,

    because their beliefs are the way they cope

    with the fear of the unknown.

Rather than face the terror of their true ignorance

    they attack that which threatens their coping mechanism.

People *identify* with their beliefs and thus identify with

    the survival effort of those beliefs as well.

Prevailing beliefs fight (quite unfairly) in order to "live."

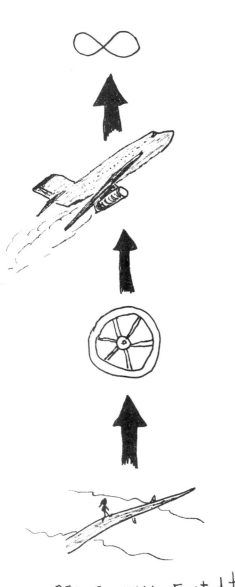

pro-SURVIVAL Fact data   prevailing belief data

And so the two types of memory data:

pro-survival fact data and **prevailing belief data,**

the **proven** and the **unproven,**

the **factual** and the **fictional,**

steadily amassed in the human mind down the ages.

The great human difficulty has been the inability to tell the difference between the true and the untrue—between, for example,

the science of metallurgy and

the "necessity" of slavery.

Facts are always pro-survival because, within limits, they accurately and consistently verify reality.

Prevailing beliefs are anti-survival because they present themselves as absolute truth when they are at best theoretical and at worst blind superstition.

The next great step of evolution, that is, the next step in the Game of God, required human beings to become aware of **THEMSELVES**.

To become self-aware was to ask the question,

"Who am I?"

The answer could only come in the form of a

prevailing belief.

7

WHO AM I?

"There are three mental states that interest me," said Amanda..."These are: one, amnesia; two, euphoria; three, ecstacy...Amnesia is not knowing who one is and wanting desperately to find out. Euphoria is not knowing who one is and not caring. Ecstacy is knowing exactly who one is—and still not caring."

—Tom Robbins, Another Roadside Attraction

"Hey, er..." said Zaphod, "what's your name?"
The man looked at them doubtfully.
"I don't know. Why, do you think I should have one? It seems very odd to give a bundle of vague sensory perceptions a name."

—Douglas Adams, The Restaurant at the End of the Universe

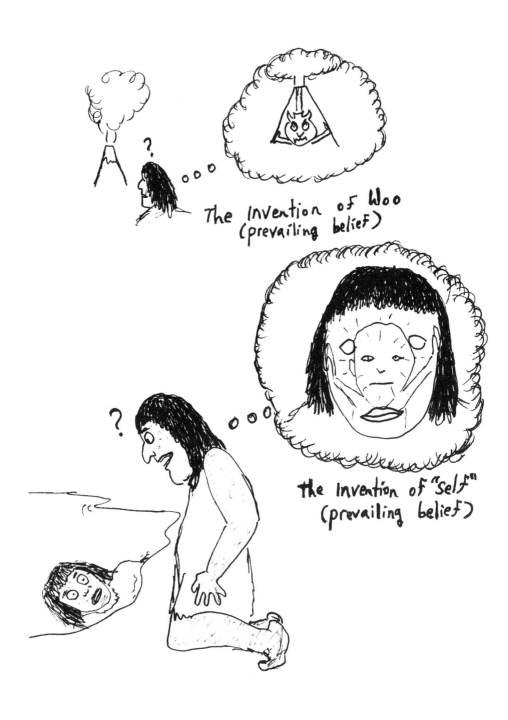

The Invention of Woo
(prevailing belief)

the Invention of "Self"
(prevailing belief)

Humans began to question not only the nature of their environment, but the nature of themselves as well.

We needed to understand the mystery of ourselves as much as the villagers needed to understand the mystery of the volcano, and we **invented ourselves** in the same way that the villagers invented the volcano god.

What we came to believe was "us," was a primary survival identity called the "ego" or "personality."

Remember that the primary survival identity of a form is defined as *the essential structure which dictates survival behavior.* In a human being, this essential structure (*who the human being **most** believes him/herself to be*) is the personality—what we call the **ego-identity**.

What is a "personality"?

We define personality as: *individual identity, as expressed in a person's behavior and attitudes.* Webster's dictionary defines *ego* as *the individual as aware of him/herself.*

The ego-identity and the personality are one and the same: *an awareness of self distinct from the physical body.* No matter how much we "identify" with our physical bodies, it is our personality/ego that we **most** identify with...and survive as.

Why self-awareness in the
womb is a bad idea.

Let's examine a human life and see how a single prevailing belief can contribute to the formation of an ego-identity: a prevailing belief system.

Let's follow the life of "Johnny."

Is a sperm or egg "self-aware"?
　No more than any other micro-organism.

Is the fetus "self-aware"?
　No more than any other animal fetus.

Self-awareness requires expanded memory storage,
　which allows us to analyze our growing memory data
and from it ***decide* who we are**,
　and then ***remember* who we decided we are.**
This processing requires a fully developed human
　brain.

The fetus's brain is not developed enough
　for the formation of prevailing beliefs
　　(which is all that the ego-identity is comprised of).

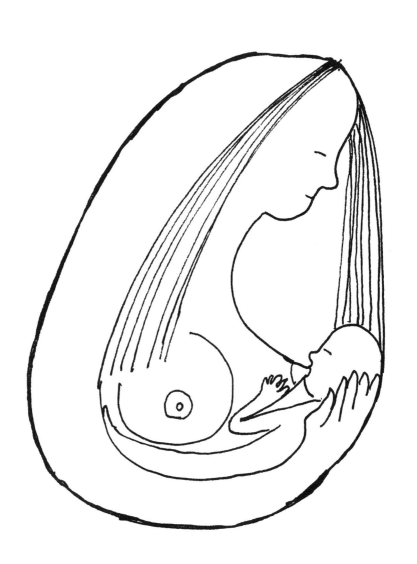

Even after birth,

it is scientifically accepted

that babies have **no sense**

of themselves as separate

from their mothers and their environment.

The duration of this state would vary

depending upon the baby's upbringing.

Intimacy with the mother during

breast-feeding, for example,

would tend to prolong this sense of oneness.

While true self-awareness

as ego-identity

is not yet attained by the baby,

the foundation for ego

has been under construction

since the fertilization event.

Remember that a belief

cannot survive on its own...

it requires a believer.

UNIVERSE	HUMAN BEING
BIG Bang	Fertilization EVENT
Formation of galaxies stars + planets	Fetal Development
Dawn OF Life KA ZAAM	BIRTH
EVOLUTION AND EDEN	Babyhood
Dawn of Homo sapiens	NO! The Dawn of ego identity the terrible twos

The development of a human being could be seen to parallel the evolution of the physical universe.

Self-awareness/ego-identity begins to appear about the second year of life.

The toddler has developed an ego-identity to the landmark extent of being able *to challenge authority—to voice an opinion.*

This activity confirms the existence of a perspective of her/himself as **distinct** and **separate** from her/his environment.

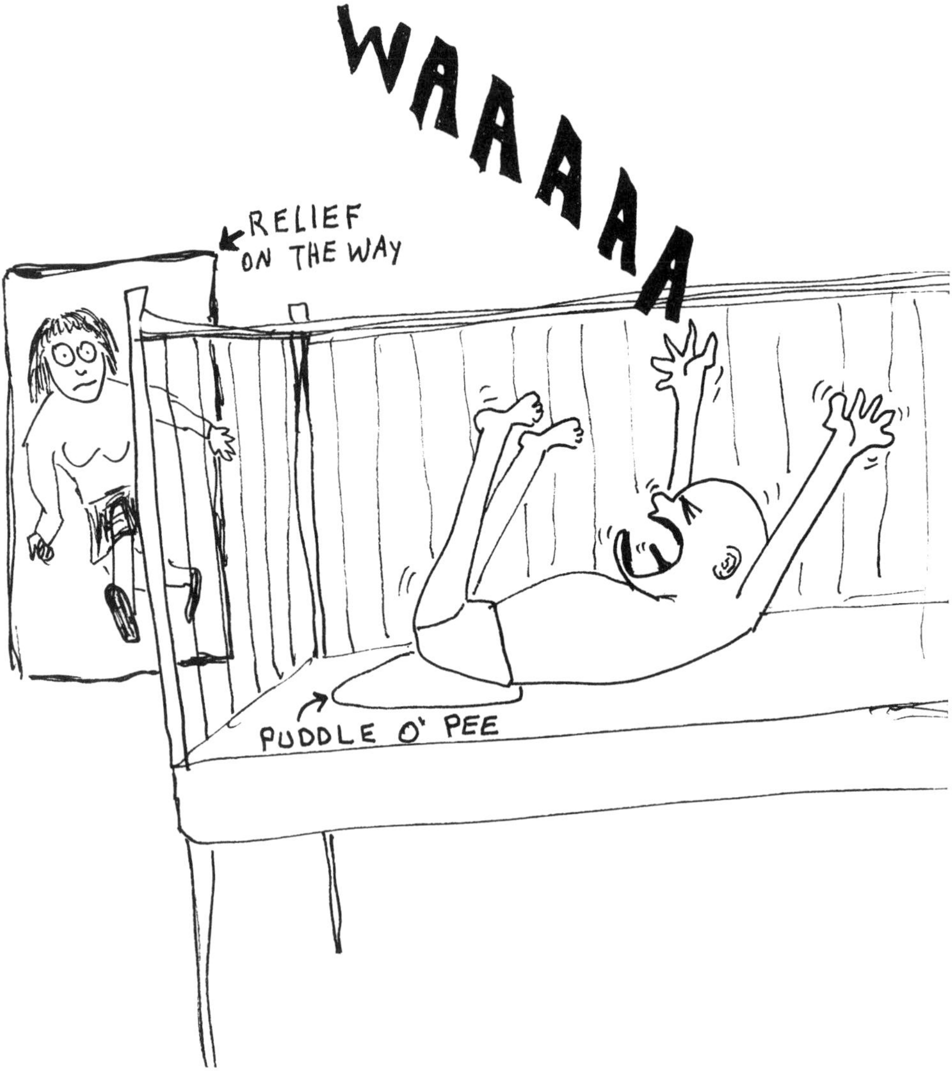
WAAAAAA
RELIEF
ON THE WAY
PUDDLE O' PEE

The development of a human's self-awareness
parallels the evolution of the non-physical universe—
the universe of **thought-forms**
(pro-survival fact data and prevailing beliefs).

Pro-survival fact data came first:
thought-forms (conclusions, beliefs, etc.) which produced
results verifiable in the physical environment and which
appeared to enhance physical survival.

For example, baby Johnny arrives at the conclusion:
"crying brings relief."

All surviving forms use the power at their disposal.

If the infant produces what she or he perceives to be pro-survival results through the shedding of tears, an association is formed based on memories of

crying = relief = comfort = survival.

As crying is an appropriate method of communication for infants, this equation is a **pro-survival fact.** Unless abandoned, however, it will become a **prevailing belief.**

After a certain age, with the exception of true grief, appreciation of beauty, etc., crying is no longer an appropriate form of communication. Instead, crying becomes a deceitful method of manipulating reality; an evasion of responsibility for one's behavior. Deceitful manipulation of reality is **anti-survival**. Remember that acceptance of reality always enhances survival. Deceitful manipulation, even when it is an unconscious process, carries a burden of guilt and self-hatred which is anti-survival. *Nevertheless, the prevailing belief, in order to survive, must convince its believer that it is pro-survival.*

"Johnny" doesn't stop crying. The prevailing belief, *crying = survival*, has become a part of the personality called "Johnny," and makes Johnny a crybaby for a lifetime. The prevailing belief, *crying produces results*, will effort to maintain structural integrity **forever.**

The **single goal** of every

belief, decision, conclusion, and association

(which together make up the ego-identity)

is **survival**,

and survival is equated with

getting one's way.

While Johnny's technique (one of many)

for getting his way

is through tears,

others may opt

for:

accomplishment,

whining,   pleasing,

illness,   flattery,

deception,   sulking,

accidents, insanity,

guilt,

etc.

The point is

that a life-long **attitude** is formed

based on what one believes to be

the best method of surviving

(the best method of getting one's way).

I'M SO SORRY! I WAS SO DRUNK I DON'T REMEMBER BEATING YOU UP! WAAAAA
It's OK Dear, I forgive you!
RESULTS

We bring people into our lives who

"buy our act"—

that is, who respond to our survival methods

and let us have our way.

It is important to notice that those people

who "let us" have our way,

are getting **us** to let **them**

have **their way** in return.

(Some people think

that being a victim

is a very good method of surviving).

Johnny, for instance,

noticed early on that *women*,

far more than men,

responded favorably to his tears.

Another association/prevailing belief was formed:

"women provide me with better service."

OLD BASTARD!
Don't Worry Dad, we'll take care of you!
Go AHEAD! put me in a home! See if I care!
WAAAAA
NO RESULTS
RESULTS

The unexamined life

takes on a certain

sameness...

A prevailing belief,
unexamined and
unchallenged,
will operate
without change
for a lifetime.

CRYING BRINGS HELP
WHICH HELPS ME TO SURVIVE.
CRYING LETS ME GET MY WAY
WHICH MAKES ME HAPPY
WHICH MAKES ME SURVIVE.
WOMEN RESPOND TO MY
TEARS MORE THAN MEN.
I AM NOT A REAL MAN
WHEN I CRY BUT I SURVIVE.
I NEED A WOMAN IN
MY LIFE WHO WILL CARE
FOR ME LIKE MY A
MOTHER. I AM A
FAILURE BUT AT
LEAST I SURVIVE

Because Johnny cries to get his way,
  and because our society believes it is unmanly
 for men to cry,
Johnny concludes that *he is weak and unmanly*.

Because Johnny believes he is weak and unmanly,
  and because society believes only strong men succeed,
Johnny concludes *he is a loser/failure*.

Because Johnny believes he is a loser/failure,
 he believes he needs someone to help him through life,
 and because some women respond to his tears
 just like his mother did,
Johnny *finds a substitute mother for his wife*.

Because Johnny believes he is weak and a failure,
  and because this is shameful in our society,
Johnny *is filled with shame*.

Because Johnny is filled with shame,
 and needs a way to suppress it,
Johnny *turns to alcohol...etc....etc....etc....etc....*

God-as-form now has a personality.

I THINK

I AM A CRYBABY, UGLY,
BEAUTIFUL, A LOSER, LAZY,
SNEAKY, A PHONEY, ETC.

THEREFORE
I AM

A CRYBABY, UGLY,
BEAUTIFUL, A LOSER, LAZY,
SNEAKY, A PHONEY, ETC.

We have just followed one prevailing belief through a lifetime. An ego-identity is comprised of innumerable prevailing beliefs, all of which arose from behavior that we as infants and toddlers concluded produced pro-survival results. Beginning as pro-survival facts, these thought-forms became prevailing beliefs when we **failed to appropriately abandon them,** and instead decided that they were "who we were," and were the way to behave in the future.

These prevailing beliefs are so powerful (being perceived and stored as matters of life and death) that in unquestioningly following them they become **literally "who we are."**

Who are we, after all, if not the sum total of our self-judgments, self-opinions, self-analyses, etc.?

Our opinions and value judgments of ourselves are exactly who we think we are. These opinions and value judgments determine all of our behavior. Our behavior becomes **entirely automatic.**

WE ALWAYS ACT LIKE "US"!

8

THE MASK OF EGO

...the mind is restless, turbulent, strong and unyielding...as difficult to subdue as the wind.
                                                    —*Bhagavad Gita*

Which of us has known his brother? Which of us has looked into his father's heart? Which of us has not remained forever prison-pent? Which of us is not forever a stranger and alone?
                            —*Thomas Wolfe, Look Homeward, Angel*

...I mingle with my peers or no one, and since I have no peers, I mingle with no one. [Ignatius J. Reilly]
                    —*John Kennedy Toole, A Confederacy of Dunces*

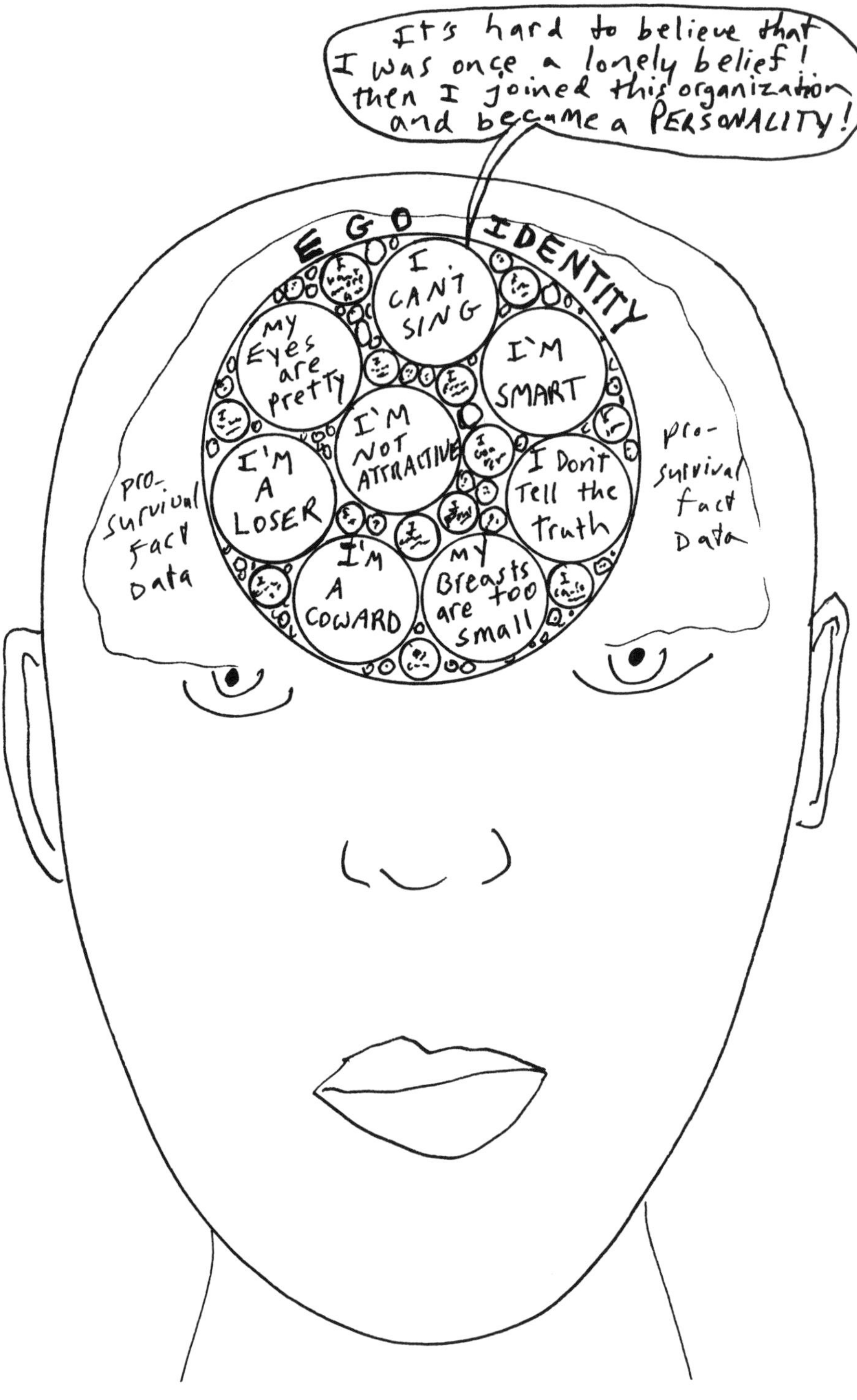
It's hard to believe that I was once a lonely belief! then I joined this organization and became a PERSONALITY!
EGO IDENTITY
I CAN'T SING
My Eyes are pretty
I'M SMART
I'M NOT ATTRACTIVE
I'M A LOSER
I Don't Tell the Truth
I'M A COWARD
My Breasts are too small
pro-survival fact Data
pro-survival fact Data

A human ego-identity

is a **thought-form**

comprised of every individual thought-form

(belief, value judgement, etc.)

one holds about oneself.

Just as any particle

which joins a community of particles

abandons its individual survival identity

for the survival identity of the community,

so does every individual prevailing belief

abandon its individual survival identity

to support the entire ego/personality,

or "*ME*."

Who "*ME*" is

is **ONE BIG**

prevailing belief.

1. Baby   2. Child

3. Teenager   4. Adult

The ego fortification

The primary survival identity

of the human being

is the ego.

The ego (personality)

is made of prevailing beliefs—

opinions we formed

about ourselves that,

in order to

survive unchanged,

must pass

themselves off

to us

as absolute truths.

The root word of personality is the Greek *persona*,

which literally means *an actor's face mask*.

Our iron masks of ego

are well under construction

before the age of two,

and the rest of our lives,

unless we challenge our masks,

are lived

behind them.

Hi, my name's Bob! God I just hate cocktail parties don't you? (attempt to impress attractive woman)
Why no, I find them perfectly delightful! (successsful attempt to squelch come on)
Flag of Hope
SNAP!
BOOM!

The blunt truth is

> **that we act as though**
>
> > **we know "who we are,"**
>
> **when the fact is**
>
> > **we haven't the faintest idea**
>
> **who, what, where, why, etc., we are.**

We think we "know" a thing when we label it.

> What is a tree? A collection of cells.
>
> What is a cell? A collection of molecules.
>
> What is a molecule? A collection of atoms.
>
> What is an atom? A collection of elementary particles.
>
> What is an elementary particle? No one has the faintest
>
> > idea— ABSOLUTE IGNORANCE.

The ego is more than clever enough to pretend to be

> humble: to say "Of course I don't know it all," when its

(our) behavior clearly says otherwise.

Our personalities were **invented**

> precisely like "Woo" was invented—
>
> > as a way of coping with **absolute ignorance**.

In fact, our masks are a variation on a theme:

> we imitated the world of ego masks
>
> > we were born into,
>
> > > and made up our own version.

Deep down, we **know** we are not our mask.

Who, after all, made up the mask?

Deep down, we know that our mask is phoney,

and we know that our personality

is built on the thin air of absolute ignorance.

Because we do not really know who we are,

we are in constant fear of

who we might or might not really be.

The unknown is the source of all fear

and anything we are afraid of we are bound to hate.

It is impossible to fear

that which one does not hate

and it is impossible to hate

that which one does not fear.

To the extent we do not know ourselves

we **fear** ourselves,

and to the extent we fear ourselves

we **hate** ourselves.

According to this formula

it should be obvious that

self-fear and self-hatred are universal.

These states exist consciously and/or unconsciously in all.

So, ya wanta get rid of me eh? Well not so fast! I got evidence, see? I can prove what a jerk you are! Want to look at some of these photos or listen to some tapes? It's all here - and unless you do as I say I'll turn it over to the cops and the papers, see?

Because we cannot
remain sane or survive
under the combined weight
of self-fear and self-hatred,
the ego allows us (for a price)
the ability to **suppress** and **repress**
the awareness of these unhappy states:
the ability to convince ourselves
that we are really "OK."

We are allowed
to promote our "strong points"
and hide our weaknesses—
from ourselves and,
we believe, from the world.
It is important to note that this process
is almost entirely **unconscious**.

The price we pay
is **ABSOLUTE OBEDIENCE**
to our Master ego ("Me"),
who threatens us with revealing
what we **really** think of ourselves,
should we ever attempt to rebel
and challenge its authority.

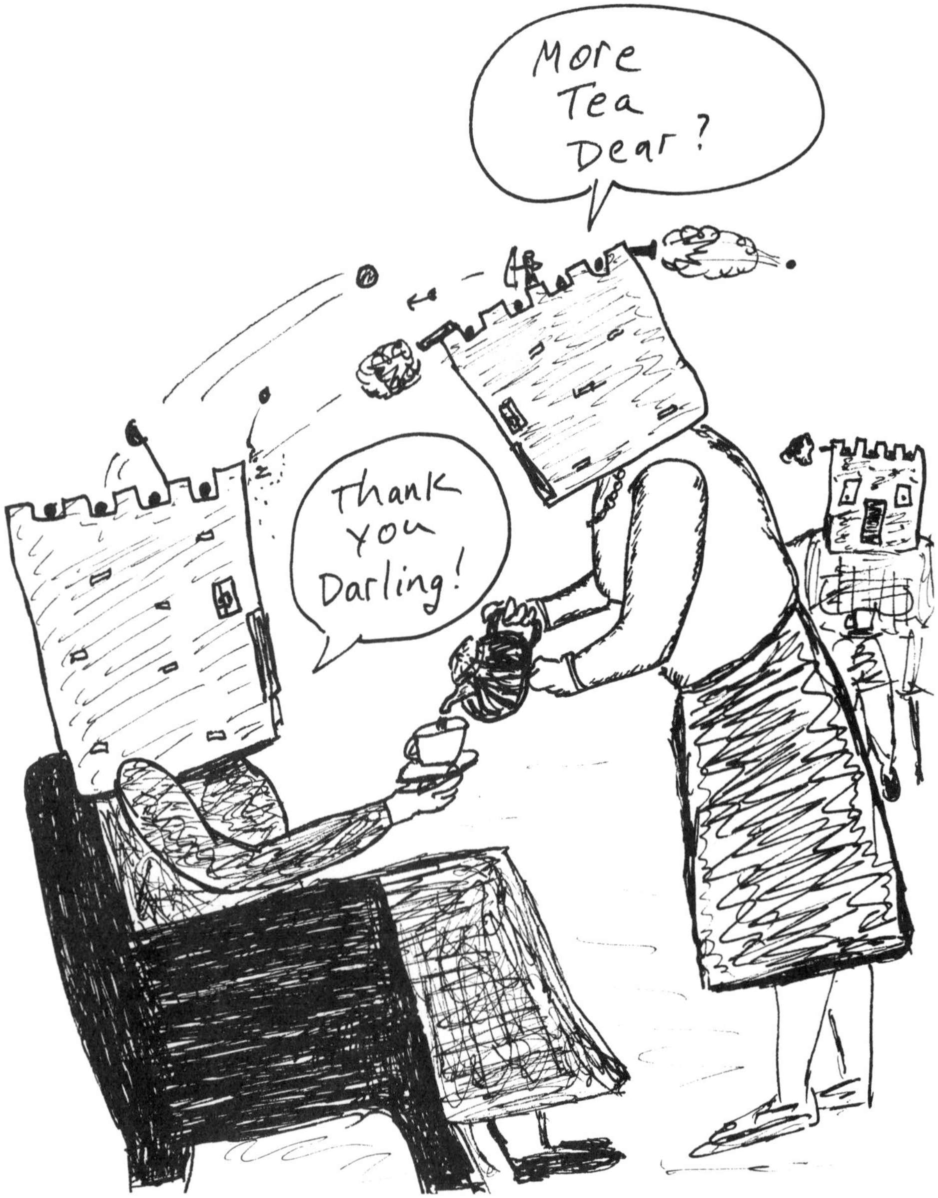
More Tea Dear?
Thank you Darling!

We are saying that all a personality can do
is flight/fear or fight/hate.

This is because a personality is nothing but a mass of
thought-forms called prevailing beliefs, which can only
effort to maintain their existent structural integrity:
to constantly attempt to remain *unchanged*.

This is the reason why human beings resist change.

All human behavior, with one exception,
is flight/fight survival behavior.

This results in a world filled with human pain.

This guy looks pretty insecure. Prepare to fire a volley of smugness and confidence!
He's going to start something! stand by to retaliate!
Yes sir! Smugness and confidence, stand by to fire!

The survival nature of the ego is such

that it is bound to be in competition and in conflict with

every other ego on Earth.

History well documents the bloody results of ego conflict.

To look at history is to invite despair.

While people have changed superficially,

humanity still operates,

with a single exception we shall shortly examine,

out of flight/fight survival behavior.

The threat of exposing ego's prevailing beliefs

as lies (opinions posing as truths)

does not come from rocks, trees, or animals

(one reason why pets are so popular).

The threat comes from other human beings.

We must constantly be on guard

to avoid penetration of our defenses.

Simultaneously, we observe and carefully catalogue

all of the faults and weaknesses

we perceive in others,

both to elevate ourselves and to gather material to be

used **offensively** in case they should choose

to attack the weaknesses and faults

they perceive in **US**.

Hello.
How do you do?
I'm very pleased to meet you!
The pleasure is all mine, I assure you!

Just as two dogs,

on meeting,

"check each other out"

and establish dominance,

so do humans

quickly size each other up.

The human race

is a glorified

pecking order.

Eternal Vigilance is the Price

01	Intelligence	
00	Education	
11	Politics	
10	sense of humor	
11	hobbies	
110	theology	
110	philosophy	
01	taste in art	
00	use of intoxicants	
011	sexual preferences	
010	background	
110	Family relationship	

Hair   01100010 10
Skin   1000 0110 04
Eyebrows 01 0/00 111
Eyes   1100 11 0010 1
Nose   001 10 110
Mouth   011 1 001 1
Teeth   00 11 00 010
Breath   11 0 01 110
Body   DATA PENDING
clothes   — "
Grooming
nails   — — "
Hands   — "
Fingers   — "
Arms   —
Ass   — " "

THE WAR ROOM

Every person,

depending upon his or her individual "psychology"

  (those variations of prevailing beliefs

   which make each ego unique)

has a list of "negatives" (faults and weaknesses)

which she or he looks for in others

in order to establish "superiority."

Whenever we meet someone,

we judge them against our standard.

Because the ego must present itself

as the absolute truth,

it must be superior to all other possible truths—

therefore superior to every other ego.

The cynic looks for the worst *consciously*.

Most of us do our fault-finding *unconsciously*—

and thus retain our "nice person" self-image.

Our ego must be number one.

Even if we meet a person who is famous, rich, etc.,

and it appears that they are "above us,"

our egos will somehow contrive to make us

superior (they were born lucky,

we didn't get the breaks, etc. etc.).

Positive = Negative
Negative = Positive

uneducated	educated
Long hair	short hair
One eye	two eyes
Smoker	non-smoker
Unkempt	Well-groomed
Tattoo	No Tattoo

BORN TO LOSE

CHUNKY   LEAN

DRINKER   Violent   PASSIVE

NON-DRINKER

CRUDE   REFINED

RUDE   POLITE

Remember

that for a belief

to continue to survive unchanged,

it must convince

the believer that

it is absolutely true.

The belief

must therefore be

convincingly

logical

to the believer.

This means

that for every

negative

on our list of dislikes,

there **must**

be an opposing

positive.

For example,

if *cursing* is held to be a "negative,"

then *not-cursing* **must** be held to be a "positive."

We have mentioned that there is a single alternative to flight(fear)/fight(hate) survival behavior.

What is it?

The key to the alternative lies in the **positive list**.

Ordinarily, the people we meet easily possess enough "negatives" for us to feel superior to them, which enables us to maintain ego's favorite defensive position:

aloof, "safe," separate, and alone.

THE GENERAL PUBLIC
Negative Negative Negative
Positive Negative Negative
Negative Positive Negative
ACQUAINTANCES
Positive Negative Positive
Negative Negative Positive
Positive Negative Negative
FRIENDS
Positive Positive Positive
Negative Positive Positive
Negative Positive Negative
BEST FRIEND
Positive positive Positive
Positive positive negative
positive positive negative

We do not accept people
who are different from us,
because of the potential threat
they offer to our prevailing beliefs.
We like to be around people who agree with us
because they do not threaten
the survival of our prevailing beliefs
as absolute truths.

A few people,
whose behavior generally conforms to
our list of positives and negatives
(and who therefore have similar tastes)
become our friends.

A smaller number,
whose behavior satisfies even more of
our positive criteria,
become our closest friends.

The process continues...

INTOLERANCE
Fear, hate, threat to survival, sight and smell of poverty and alcoholic panhandler is repulsive and uncomfortable due to negative and superficial value judgments. Response: ignore, move away - thinking "get a job you worthless bum."
ACCEPTANCE
Human being in need - clear signs of alcohol addiction Realize that NO ONE would willingly choose to suffer so... this person is ill. Response: Unlimited possibilities.
spare any change lady?

What is happening is simply a process of

accepting those who conform to our tastes.

We accept our best friend more than

we accept our friends.

We accept our friends more than

we accept our acquaintances.

We accept our acquaintances more than

we accept strangers on the street.

When we do not accept people,

we are expressing **intolerance** with the way they are.

Flight/fight survival behavior

is *a constant expression of intolerance*

with existent (present) reality.

We are always fighting against or running from reality because reality contains the forces of change which threaten our ability to maintain structural integrity.

The lone alternative to flight/fight is

the experience of accepting reality the way it is.

The experience of accepting reality the way it is

is our definition of

LOVE.

PART THREE

WINNING

THE GAME

Blessed are the poor in spirit, for theirs is the kingdom of heaven.
Blessed are those who mourn, for they shall be comforted.
Blessed are the meek, for they will inherit the earth.
Blessed are those who hunger and thirst for righteousness, for they will be filled.
Blessed are the merciful, for they will be shown mercy.
Blessed are the pure in heart, for they will see God.
Blessed are the peacemakers, for they will be called children of God.
Blessed are those who are persecuted because of righteousness, for theirs is the kingdom of heaven.
Blessed are you when people insult you, persecute you and falsely say all kinds of evil against you because of me.
Rejoice and be glad, because great is your reward in heaven, for in the same way they persecuted the prophets who were before you.

—Jesus, The Sermon on the Mount

9

LOVE

The first truth is that existence is suffering.
The second truth is that our pain and suffering are caused by
what we perceive to be our human needs and cravings.
The third truth is that our pain and suffering can end if we
learn to eliminate our human needs and cravings.
The fourth truth is that continual practice of the eightfold path
will lead to the cessation of all suffering and to a life that is
serene and free.

—the Buddha, Four Noble Truths

With all beings and all things we shall be as relatives.

—Sioux Indian

I still believe that people are really good at heart.

—Anne Frank, The Diary of Anne Frank

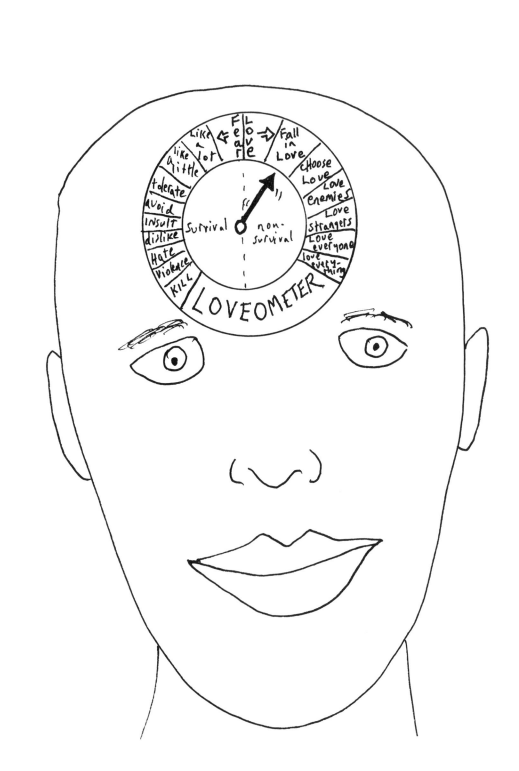

We define love as

> *the experience of unconditional acceptance*
> *of what is.*

Love is EXPERIENCE.

We define experience as

> *being, free of a survival identity.*

Studying these two definitions, we see that

> **love is the experience which surfaces**
> > **in direct proportion**
> > > **to the absence of flight/fight survival identity**.

> > When we "fall in love," for example,
> > all that has happened
> > is that we have met someone
> > who conforms to a critical number of items
> > on our "positive-trait" list.
> > When we see enough of what we deem to be
> > positive traits in others,
> > we find ourselves
> > *accepting them as they are.*
> > **That which we find acceptable**
> > **is never perceived as a threat and thus**
> > **requires no survival response on our part.**

This is the war room! This woman appears to be no threat! Begin to lower force fields, cease firing and terminate hostilities. Go to minimum alert!
This man is very agreeable and highly acceptable — reduce all defenses and acts of aggression at once — this is the war room!

We maintain our defensive posture against "*negatives*" because we perceive anything negative (unpleasant) as **anti-survival**. "*Positives*" are interpreted as **pro-survival** and therefore are openly welcomed—no survival effort is required. We drop our flight/fight negativity in the experience of acceptance, and we call this experience "love."

The reason we make such a fuss over "falling in love" is because the experience is so rare—which demonstrates how much of our lives are lived behind our flight/fight survival fortifications.

"Falling in love" is a phrase which perfectly describes how the experience of love takes us by surprise. We "fall" in love via an unconscious process:
  (a) we have a picture in our minds of the *"perfect person,"*
  (b) we meet someone who comes close to that perfect image,
  (c) we *automatically* lower our defenses, and
  (d) we experience love.

We do not choose love when we *fall* in it:
  love happens to us involuntarily.

Down with El supremo!
VIVa la revolution!
Freedom!
liberty!
Love
ego
El Supremo
TRUST NO ONE (except me)
Grrr... I'll be back!

The experience of love is like an internal revolution: the ego-identity tyrant is momentarily overthrown. The joy of love is the result of sudden liberation from the incessant fear and hatred of dictated survival behavior. In the experience of love the world takes on a fresh appearance, because the world is no longer perceived through a filter of survival defenses. Life seems exactly right, and actually worth living for a change.

Because the ego-identity is a survival machine, the experience of love is naturally perceived as the ultimate threat. Flighting or fighting is all an ego can do, and both of these behaviors are expressions of intolerance with the way it is. Love is acceptance of the way it is. Thus for ego to regain control, which by Universal Law it must attempt to do, it will reintroduce intolerance and destroy acceptance.

One of the first expressions of intolerance which will destroy the love experience is the fear that the love will go away. From this fear comes possessiveness, jealousy, etc.

As no one can exactly match our positive list, it is only a matter of time until ego regains enough control to start rooting out the negative traits in the person we, for a time, experienced as "perfect." Ego will even cynically question the sincerity of another saying "I love you" (remember that self-hatred is universal). EGO IS THE KILLER OF LOVE.

What is love?

It is a common belief that there are many "types" of love.

We think there is only ONE:
　the experience of unconditional acceptance of what is.

The reason there *appears* to be different types of love
　is due to human misinterpretation:
　　beliefs, labeling,
　　rules, and misunderstanding.

Love comes from one source.

INFINITY

love

love

love

love

love

love

NON-PHYSICAL Realm

PHYSICAL

THOUGHTS,
EMOTIONS,
+
FEELINGS

love

love

love

love

love

love

S
I
C
A
L

R
E
A
L
M

love

love

love

love

love

INFINITY

love

"But if love is acceptance, which occurs in the absence of flight/fight survival behavior, what is it? Are not the first two Laws of the Universe: 1. exist as form and 2. survive as form?"

EXACTLY.

LOVE IS NOT A FORM.

Love is not a physical or non-physical surviving form.

LOVE IS NOT AN EMOTION OR FEELING.

Emotions and feelings are produced by non-physical surviving thought-forms and by the physical surviving form.

LOVE IS NOT AN INTELLECTUAL PROCESS.

Intellectual processes are produced by non-physical surviving thought-forms and by the physical surviving form.

Feelings, emotions, and thoughts can **register** and **react to** the experience of love,

but they should never be confused **with** the experience of love.

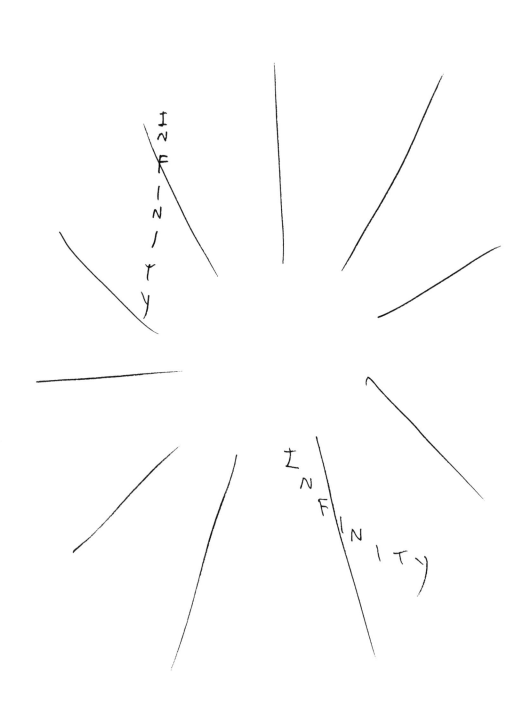

Love is **unconditional acceptance** of what is.

  Acceptance is the alternative to flight/fight,

    it is not survival behavior.

      Love does not have to survive

        because it is **ETERNAL**.

  Unconditional means "without limits."

    Love is, ultimately, an *ABSOLUTE experience.*

      Love is, ultimately, **ABSOLUTELY UNLIMITED**.

        Love is absolute acceptance of absolute reality.

Love is the Second Purpose of the Universe Game—

  for the limited to experience the unlimited—

    being realized.

Love is God...and God is Love.

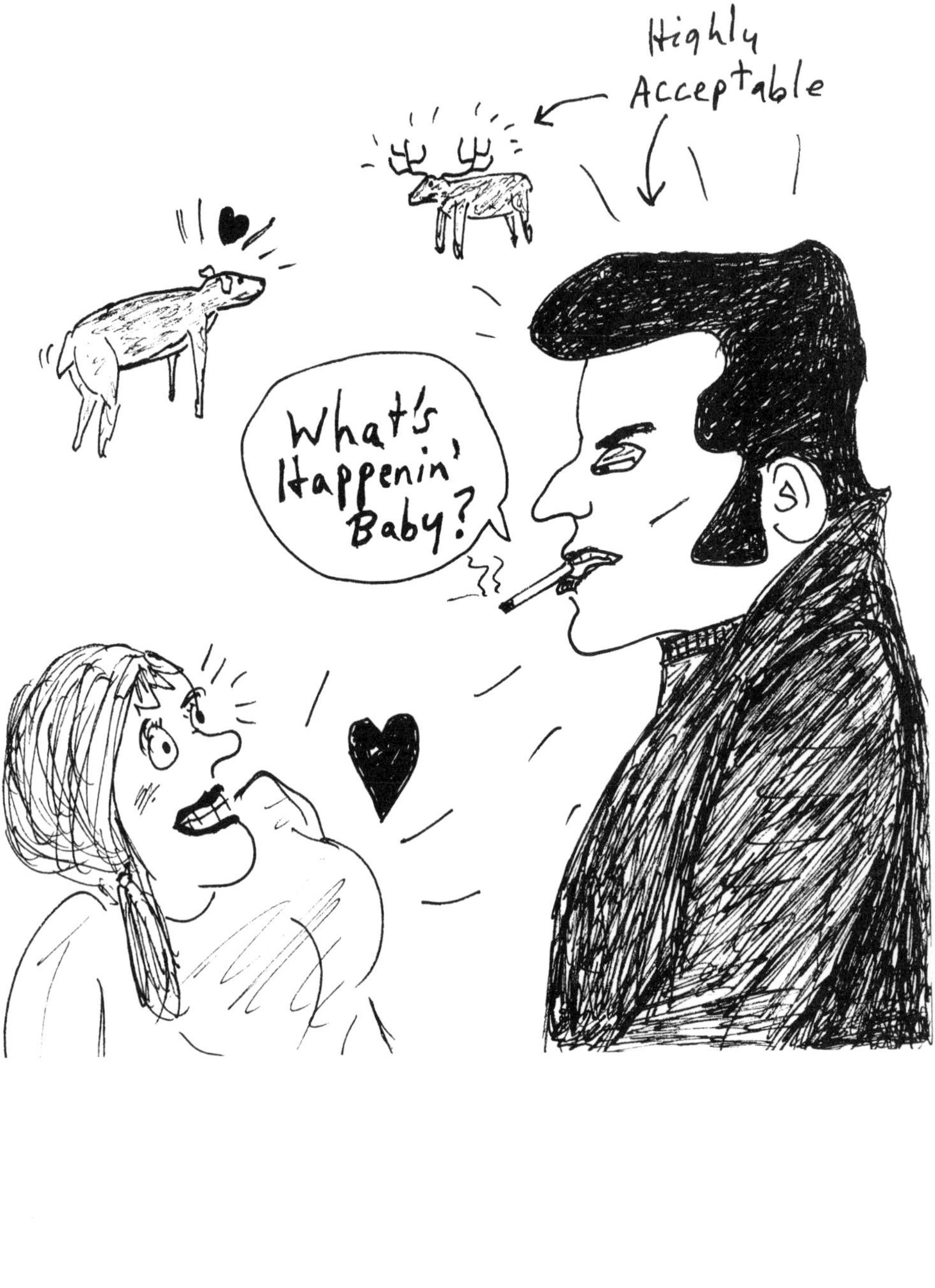
Highly Acceptable
What's Happenin' Baby?

Those who have
experienced love
have experienced,
whether they know it or not,
God-consciousness surfacing
into their awareness.

The rudiments of this surfacing
can be found in the animal kingdom.
Animals "accept" mates,
sometimes for life
(if this were not the case,
animals could never let down
their flight/fight defenses
and come together to reproduce).

The difference
between humans and other animals
is that while humans largely behave
exactly like animals—accepting a mate
based upon a list of positive traits
(*big antlers, big eyes, or big bank account*)—
humans have the unique
and largely undiscovered potential
to **CHOOSE LOVE**.

I don't like the shape of the sun,* I don't like the color of oranges,* I don't like gravity,* I don't like the wetness of water,* I don't...
I don't like people who drink,* I don't like people who smoke,* I don't like people who curse,* I don't like people who don't believe the way I do,* I don't like people who dress funny,* I don't like people who are INTOLERANT*!
I don't like insane people* either!
"INSANE" person
"NORMAL" person
*Reality

"How could humans choose love?"

Looking at our definition of love

we see that love, as acceptance of what is,

is nothing more or less

than **the acceptance of reality.**

The accurate perception

and acceptance of reality

is surely a definition of

mental health.

The experience of love

is the true definition of

mental health.

This should explain

why the human race

often acts as though it were insane—

IT IS.

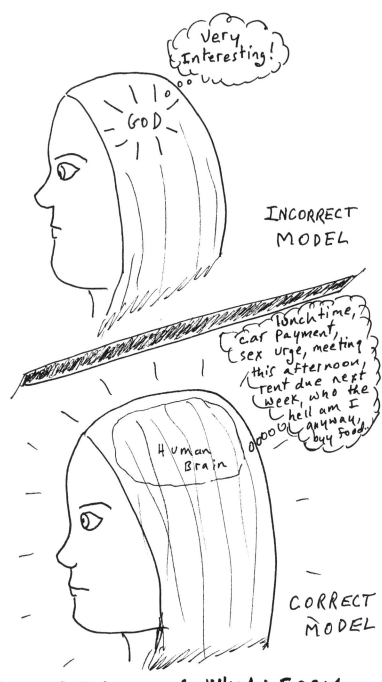

GOD EXPERIENCING HUMAN FORM

This human "insanity" was of course

   planned by the Creator—

"insanity" being the inability

   to accurately perceive and/or accept reality.

This temporary state of "insanity,"

   created via amnesia,

is the **only conceivable way** that

   the Unlimited could experience limitation.

As long as we humans are identifying with form,

   physical or non-physical,

we can only **survive** as form.

Reality guarantees the change/death of all form,

   thus in order to survive

we must constantly struggle against

   the reality that is killing

who we think we are.

Therefore,

   as long as we identify with form,

we can only choose survival...we cannot choose love.

SURVIVAL IS THE DESTROYER OF LOVE.

To CHOOSE love means to choose God.
GOD AND LOVE ARE ONE.

God is *the absolute awareness and*
absolute acceptance of
absolute reality.
God is *the absolute experience of*
absolute reality.
God is *pure experience.*
God is *Being, free of a survival identity.*

Human beings were evolved to choose God
(the limited experiencing the unlimited),
a step which requires
the discovery and implementation
of the Third Law of the Universe:
transcend survival as form.

10

TRANSCENDING SURVIVAL AS FORM

A child said, What is the grass? *fetching it to me with full
hands;*
*How could I answer the child? I do not know what it is
anymore than he.*

—Walt Whitman, Song of Myself

Knowing ignorance is strength.
Ignoring knowledge is sickness.

If one is sick of sickness, then one is not sick.
The sage is not sick because he is sick of sickness.
Therefore he is not sick.

Lao-Tsu, Tao Te Ching

"The master said, 'Yu, shall I teach you what knowledge is?
When you know a thing, to recognize that you know it, and
when you do not know a thing, to recognize that you do not
know it. That is knowledge.'"

—Analects of Confucius

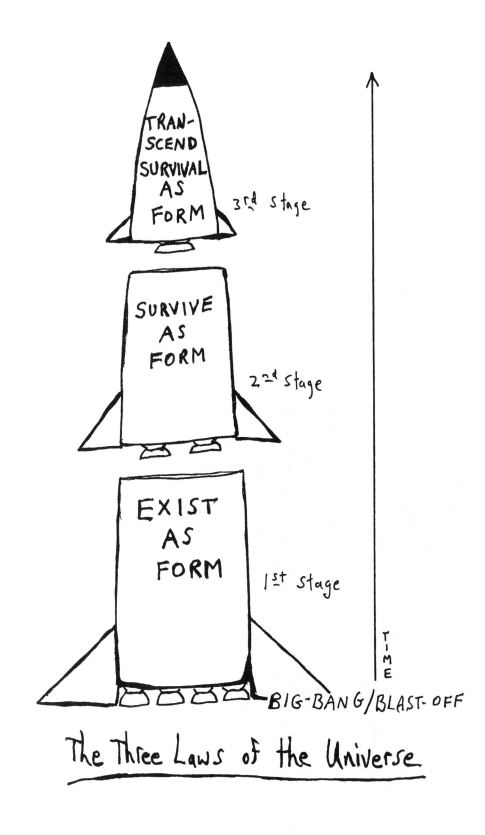

TRAN-
SCEND
SURVIVAL
AS
FORM

3rd stage

SURVIVE
AS
FORM

2nd stage

EXIST
AS
FORM

1st stage

TIME

BIG-BANG/BLAST-OFF

The Three Laws of the Universe

Let's review the Game of God and
the first two purposes of the Game.

1. *For the unlimited to experience limitation.*
We have seen how this has been accomplished
via self-induced amnesia. From the big bang
to human beings, God-as-form has evolved from total
unconsciousness to self-awareness.
2. *For the limited to experience the unlimited.*
We have seen how this purpose is realized in the
experience of love (love and God are One). This
purpose is further fulfilled when God-self-imprisoned-as-
form "discovers God," enters into "relationship with
God," and begins to escape the cage of limitation. This
is the process of God rediscovering Godself.

God has experienced limitation
via the first two Laws of the Universe:
exist as form and survive as form.
In order to fully experience the second purpose of the Game
it is now time to discover and implement
the Third Law of the Universe:

transcend survival as form.

process of
detachment

Ceasing to identify
with a form called
"Titanic"

*"What does **transcend survival as form** mean?"*

Webster's dictionary defines **transcend** as:
to go beyond the limits of;
to be separate from or beyond.

We can thus interpret this Law as meaning
a process of willful detachment from form:
that is, ceasing to identify with form
(because to identify with form
is to unsuccessfully attempt
to survive as form).

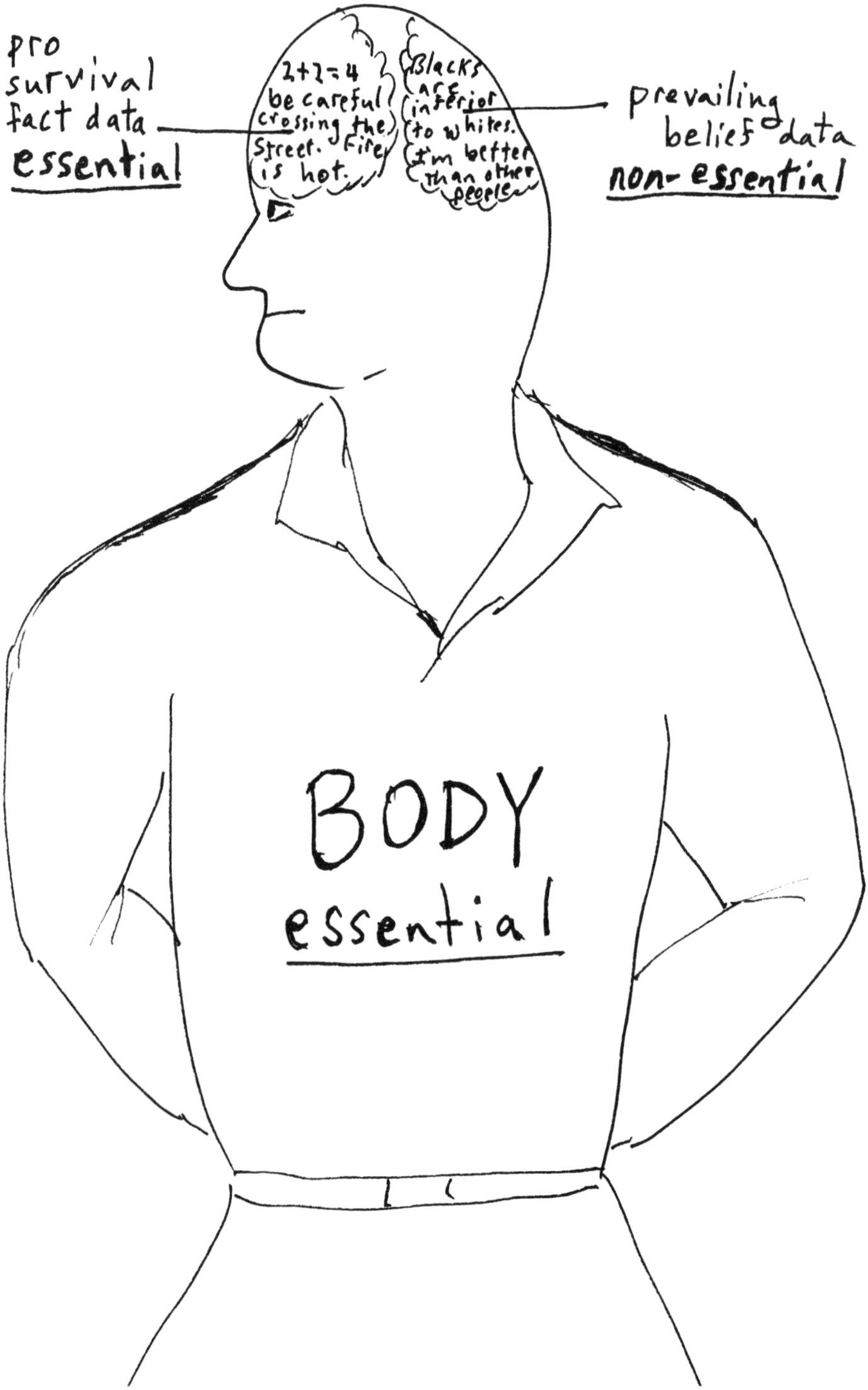
pro survival fact data
essential
2+2=4 be careful crossing the street. Fire is hot.
Blacks are inferior to whites. I'm better than other people
prevailing belief data
non-essential
BODY
essential

*But cease to identify with **what** form? With physical form—our bodies?"*

No, because to do that would be to die or disappear, and thus there would be no experience of the limited experiencing the unlimited.

"Then should we cease to identify with the pro-survival fact data thought-forms?"

No, because to do that would reduce us to the level of helpless infants—a survival-threatening situation which would again block the experience of the limited experiencing the unlimited.

There is only one category of form left. **Only by ceasing to identify with this particular form can we have the experience of the limited experiencing the unlimited.**

This expendable form is the giant prevailing belief system called the ego-identity.

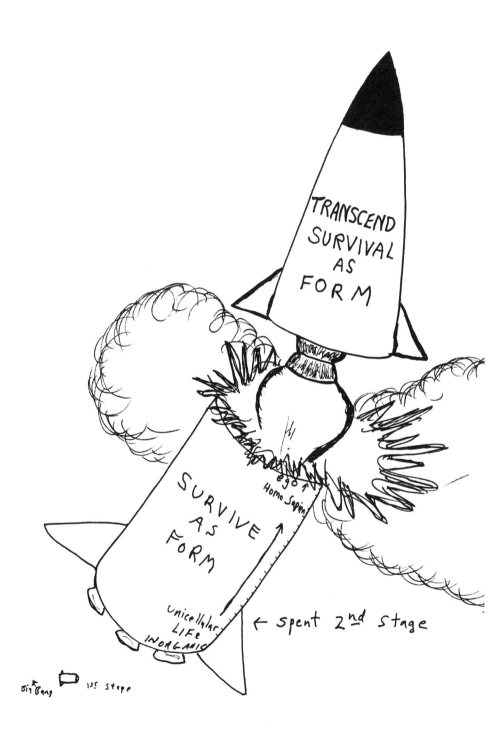

THIS IS WHY non-physical thought-forms and ego-identity were evolved.

In order to satisfy the Third Law of the Universe a primary survival identity was required that could be **renounced** and **transcended** without resulting in the death of the organism or the diminishment of the organism's consciousness.

THIS MEANS THAT THE EGO-IDENTITY,
AS AN *EXPENDABLE* SURVIVAL IDENTITY,
IS ESSENTIAL
IN THE REAWAKENING OF GOD.

Human beings were evolved to **challenge** and **renounce** their primary survival identity—the ego-identity—and thereby take the next great step in the Game.

To advance in the play we must give up our most precious possession: our entrenched idea that who we are is our personality.

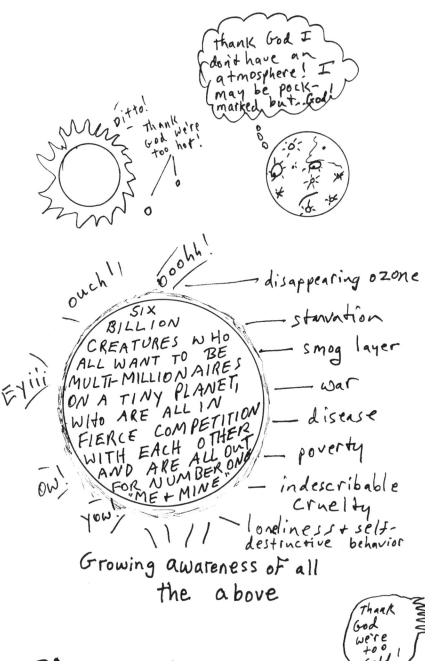

Planet of The Egos

"What is the incentive for human beings
to challenge and renounce their ego-identities?
Why should they want to?"

> The incentive is the same as that which
> has driven all evolution since the beginning
> of the universe: **existence as form is painful.**

Let us recall our definition of survival:
the effort of a specific form
to maintain its existent structural integrity.

> We have seen that this effort is futile.
> No **form** survives unchanged through time,
> with the exception of unexamined
> and unchallenged thought-forms.
> **This futile survival effort is painful.**
> Evolution has been driven by the desire
> to escape chaos, frustration, and pain.

Every step in evolution occurred because
the pain/stress of the "old way"
of behaving became intolerable.
The incentive to take the next step in evolution
is no different.
Human pain has reached an intolerable level.

Evolution could be seen

    as the attempt to escape

        the pain of survival as form.

The implementation of the Third Law of the Universe,

        transcend survival as form,

    requires a creature sufficiently evolved

        to experience reality to the extent of

            realizing the impossibility of escaping pain.

Humans were evolved

    to confront the ultimate horror:

        survival as form is utterly impossible.

EXISTENCE AS FORM IS INTOLERABLE
BECAUSE
SURVIVAL AS FORM IS IMPOSSIBLE.

The survival goal of any **physical** form

could only be changelessness/immortality

(eternal and absolute preservation

of existent structural integrity).

The survival goal of any **non-physical** form

could only be changelessness/immortality

(eternal and absolute preservation

of existent "structural" integrity).

Humans were evolved to discover that no physical form can

achieve changelessness.

This discovery is painful.

Humans were evolved to discover that all non-physical

thought-forms are limited by absolute ignorance and are

"changeless" only when they *pretend* to their host that

they are the absolute truth (which makes them lies).

This discovery is also painful.

The truth hurts, it is said, and what it hurts is the lie.

Humans were evolved to discover that in spite of all their

efforts and all their accomplishments,

they are, in fact, **dying ignoramuses**.

Ignoramus is defined as *a vain pretending to knowledge*.

Being ignorant does not make one an ignoramus: it is

pretending to know when one does not that makes one

an ignoramus. **A thought-form can *only* pretend.**

DEATH INSANITY

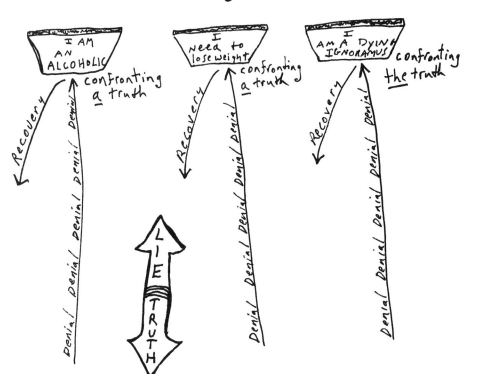

I AM
AN
ALCOHOLIC

I
need to
lose weight

I
AM A DYING
IGNORAMUS

confronting
a truth

confronting
a truth

confronting
the truth

Recovery

Recovery

Recovery

Denial Denial Denial Denial

Denial Denial Denial Denial

Denial Denial Denial Denial

LIE

TRUTH

THREE Turning Points

**Recognizing
ourselves as
dying ignoramuses
is the incentive
to transcend
survival as form.**
Evolution has worked
for billions of years
to produce a life form
sophisticated enough
to confront the truth that
it is a dying ignoramus
and a hopeless case.
The written history
of the human race
documents humanity's
attempt to escape
confronting this truth:
through conquest, blind superstition,
power, money, fame, religion,
scientific exploration, intoxicants,
philosophy, etc.

EGO
HUMANITY
ooo
come on! you can do it! The solution is just around the corner! Keep going!
Self-extinction
HUMAN HISTORY

The reason that modern life

seems to clearly be getting worse

(as the news confirms daily)

is that our efforts

to escape confronting the awful truth

of our dying ignoramus status

are virtually exhausted.

The industrial and technological revolutions

have, in a sense,

mass-produced our follies

and brought incredibly painful pressure

to bear on humankind and the planet,

to the point of actually threatening us

with self-extinction.

Pollution, environmental destruction,

overpopulation, doomsday weaponry,

and the dawning realization that

money really *can't* buy happiness,

are all pushing us toward the

Great Confrontation.

We can no longer escape the pain.

America is one of the richest and most powerful nations in the history of the world.

Yet what developed country could match this young nation in violence, in unhappiness, in prison population, in drug and alcohol abuse, or in the breakdown of the family structure?

This social experiment—once seen as the hope of humankind—is clearly not living up to the promises of humanism, science, technology, or materialism. Conventional religion seems to offer little help.

Something is missing.

It is time for the human race to stop
   trying to "fix the unfixable."
It is time to stop
   trying to make survival as form "tolerable."
It is time to stop
   denying and suppressing and running from pain.
It is time to face
   the reality of the pain and make it disappear.
It is time to embrace
   the Third Law of the Universe.
IT IS TIME TO TRANSCEND SURVIVAL AS FORM.

11

HUMANS
ANONYMOUS

Half measures availed us nothing. We stood at the turning point.

—Alcoholics Anonymous, The Big Book

Give me thy mind and give me thy heart, give me thy offerings and thy adoration; and thus with thy soul in harmony, and making me thy goal supreme, thou shalt in truth come to me.

—Bhagavad Gita

Jesus replied: "'Love the Lord your God with all your heart and with all your soul and with all your mind.' This is the first and greatest commandment. And the second is like it:'Love your neighbor as yourself.' All the Law and the Prophets hang on these two commandments."

—Matthew 22:37-40

CHOOSE ONE:

INTOLERANCE

FLIGHT FLIGHT FLIGHT FIGHT FLIGHT
effort to maintain existent structural FIGHT
FLIGHT
FLIGHT FIGHT
FIGHT
FIGHT FLIGHT integrity perpetual FIGHT FLIGHT

EGO IDENTITY

FEAR   HATRED

ACCEPTANCE

INFINITY

the experience of unconditional acceptance of what is

BEING

INFINITY

LOVE

$$\frac{\text{state of awareness}}{\text{THE ABSOLUTE PRESENT}}$$
(NO Time)

We have shown that

the primary survival identity of human beings

is the ego,

and that human beings primarily survive as their egos.

To survive as ego means to be

perpetually and reflexively obedient

to the flight/fight commands of the ego.

To survive as ego means to be

dominated by ego.

We have also shown that love

is the only alternative to flight/fight survival,

and that as long as we are identifying with ego

the best we can expect are rare, brief, and

involuntary experiences of love.

Only by willfully renouncing the ego

(ceasing to identify with it)

can we ever attain love **volitionally.**

Two questions present themselves:

how do I renounce my ego and

what would life look like without it?

We will address the first question in this chapter.

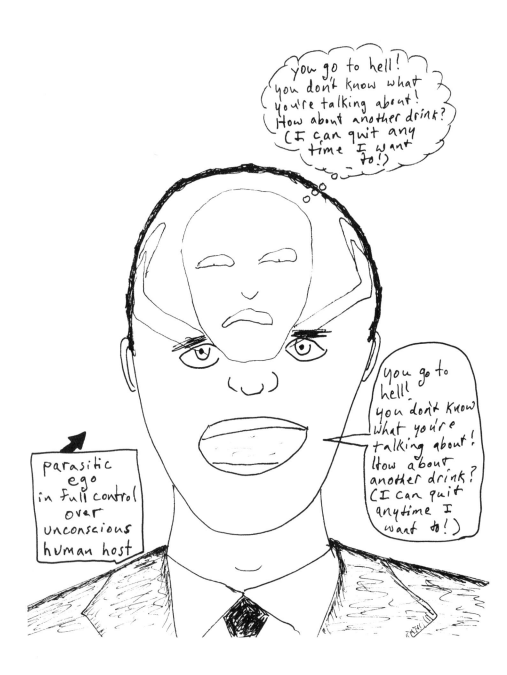

"How do I renounce my ego?"

The approach we recommend is based upon the inspired twelve-step recovery program of Alcoholics Anonymous. We are just as helplessly enslaved by our egos as alcoholics are by alcohol. In fact, ego-domination is the source of alcoholism, drug addiction, and all human suffering.

Practicing these steps **sincerely** will initiate and escalate the awakening process. These twelve steps are the essential framework for self-liberation. Other paths are available but they must include the heart of these twelve steps in order to be effective. **These steps are the *essence* of all true spiritual paths.**

The first and crucial step requires that we face the pain and the hopelessness of ego-domination (if you don't think you're dominated by your ego-identity, go back and review), and admit the exact nature of the problem.

STEP ONE:
WE ADMITTED THAT WE WERE POWERLESS OVER OUR EGOS, THAT OUR LIVES HAD ALWAYS BEEN UNMANAGEABLE.

you'll be killed! Your life isn't so bad! Leave well enough alone- tomorrow's another day! I'll let you quit smoking!
Look how long you've tried to fix your life! It's obvious you can never do it! Why not consider a power greater than yourself?
Pro-survival Fact Data-Logical conclusion
Prevailing Beliefs FIGHTING TO SURVIVE

The next step

requires us to see

that if love (mental health)

is our goal,

then we must cease

to be ego-dominated.

As long as we identify with ego,

ego will interpret our attempts

to renounce it as

killing "ourselves."

To prevent its "death,"

ego will try to convince us

that it can "fix itself."

Ego can never "fix itself"

to the point of being able

to produce love/sanity,

because love does not come from ego.

Love must come from a source

other than the body, mind, or personality.

STEP TWO:

CAME TO BELIEVE THAT A POWER GREATER THAN

OURSELVES COULD LEAD US TO SANITY.

The Higher Power cannot be another "form" (person, group, or object—real or imagined), because all form is **bound to survive** and therefore cannot be the source of love which leads one to sanity.

The Higher Power cannot be intellectually reduced to any specific "thing," or understood by a definition.

The Higher Power must be free of the limitations of form-identity in order to be considered "higher" (otherwise it is just another surviving form).

The Higher Power must be *Being, free of a survival identity*...which is our definition of *experience*.

THE HIGHER POWER IS PURE EXPERIENCE.

We use the word "God" because we are all familiar with it. We should never imagine that **using** the word "God" (or "Buddha," "Allah," "Tao," etc.) means that we **understand** God. "Understanding" blocks experience.

We only "understand" God to the degree that we **experience** God, and we are experiencing God to the exact extent to which we are experiencing love.

STEP THREE:
MADE A DECISION TO TURN OUR WILL AND
OUR LIVES OVER TO THE CARE OF GOD
AS WE UNDERSTOOD GOD.

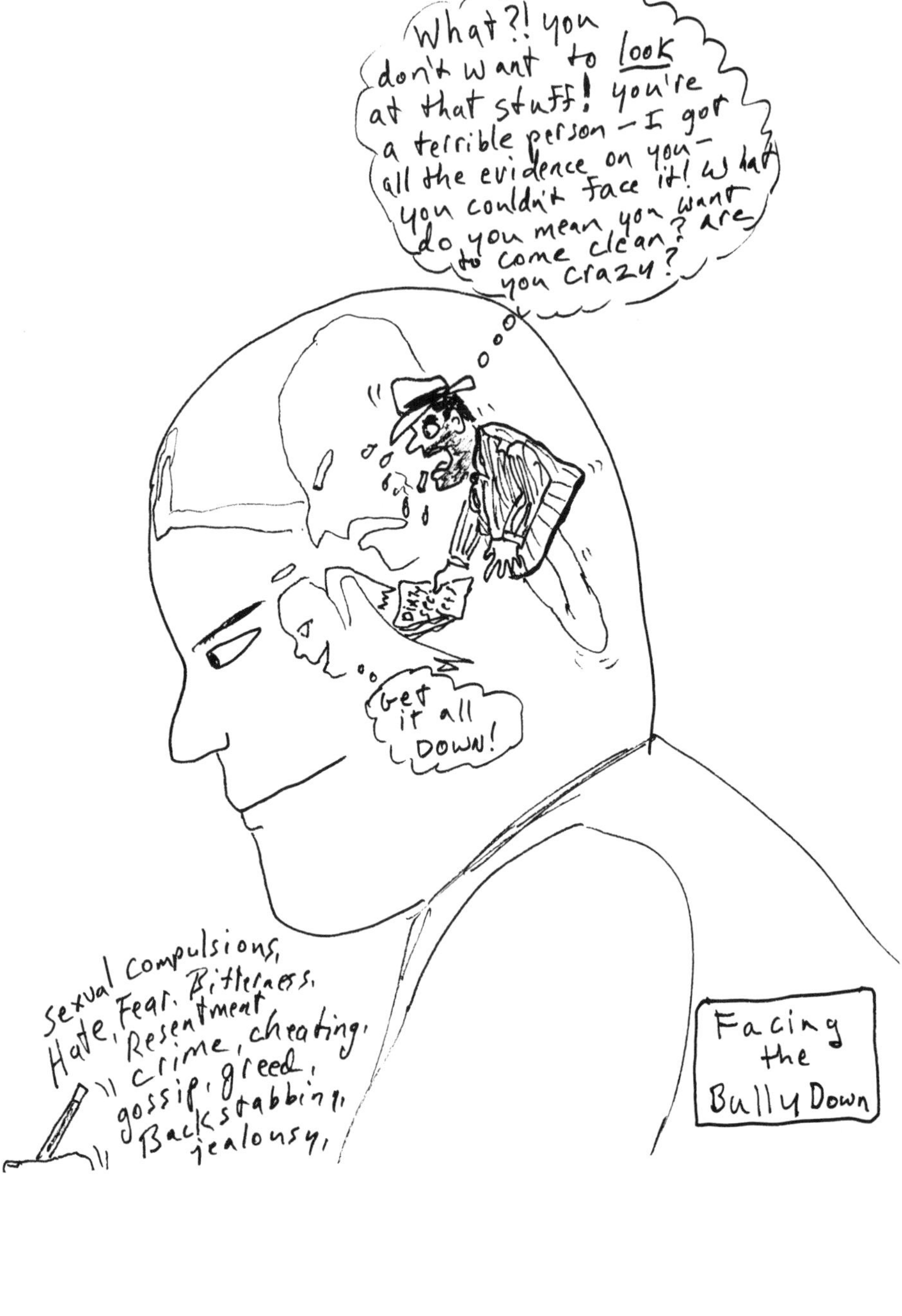
What?! you don't want to look at that stuff! you're a terrible person — I got all the evidence on you — you couldn't face it! What do you mean you want to come clean? are you crazy?
Get it all DOWN!
sexual compulsions, Hate, Fear, Bitterness, Resentment, crime, cheating, gossip, greed, Backstabbing, jealousy,
Facing the Bully Down

Now that we have made this decision

to turn our lives over to God,

we need to prepare to take this great step.

We can only be strengthened in our resolve

to turn our will and our lives over to God

by knowing exactly what it is we are "turning over."

This means facing the cruel truth

of what our lives look like

under "our" management...

under ego-domination.

STEP FOUR:
MADE A SEARCHING AND FEARLESS
MORAL INVENTORY OF OURSELVES
AS EGO-DOMINATED CREATURES.

AVOIDING suppressing DENYING Hiding shielding pretending Lying Deceiving conning concealing deluding

ARROGANCE

Not Facing It

TRUTH

Facing It

What we are working on

is the process of attaining *humility*—

a setting aside of our arrogant **lies**:

that we know what we are doing,

that we are satisfied with the way we are,

and that we don't need help from anyone.

Humility is achieved by sufficiently experiencing the **truth**:

that we *don't* know what we are doing,

that we are *not* satisfied with the way we are,

and that we are desperately in need of help.

STEP FIVE:

ADMITTED TO GOD, TO OURSELVES,

AND TO ANOTHER HUMAN BEING

THE EXACT NATURE

OF OUR EGO-DOMINATED BEHAVIOR.

In order to take the next step,

we must be experiencing true contrition

(one reason for the importance of

communicating to another human being).

We must feel that our pride is broken.

We must see our lives as such disasters that

the pain of staying as we are is intolerable.

We must experience the pain of our ego-dominated

behavior to the point of overcoming the fear

and the embarrassment of *sincerely* calling

upon the unknown for relief. *This will be the*

only step of blind faith we will ever need to

take. After this, faith will be backed up by

experience.

STEP SIX:
WERE ENTIRELY READY FOR GOD
TO REPLACE OUR EGOS
AS THE DIRECTOR OF OUR LIVES.

I Need your help absolutely God(TRUTH). you alone are the source of love and peace (TRUTH). I am a dying ignoramus filled with pride (TRUTH). you alone can save me from myself (TRUTH).
TRUTH
TRUTH
TRUTH
INFINITY
The experience of God, liberated from the imprisoning insanity of ego identity and form survival identity. God IS TRUTH!
Infinity
TRUTH
Kneeling Optional but not a bad idea!!

This step is the Main Event.

If, after taking this step,

we do not have the undeniable experience

of the presence of God

(the experience of liberation from ego-identity),

it simply means

that we did not really take the step

(we did not take it

with true humility,

which means we did not

relinquish our egos...

we need to

go back and tell more truth).

STEP SEVEN:

HUMBLY ASKED GOD

TO ASSUME FULL CONTROL OF OUR LIVES.

1. Never paid back money I borrowed from my parents.

2. am holding a lot of anger towards my ex-husband.

3. Left unpaid bills in the town I used to live in.

4. Never told my sister that I stole money from her as a child.

5.

If we have followed the first seven steps with humility and sincerity, we have now made undeniable experiential contact with God. This experience has proven the existence of a reality vastly superior to that which we have known under ego.

Ego-identity, naturally, is entirely threatened by this event, and will do everything in its power to regain control.

The purpose of the next two steps is to break up our old patterns of behavior. First, by having us face our ego-controlled past and clean up the messes we made. Second, by recreating the experience of humility to counter ego's inevitable attempts to destroy our new-found relationship with God.

To face and take responsibility for our past is to experience forgiveness for our past—thus robbing our egos of their blackmailing power over us.

STEP EIGHT:
HAVING HAD A SPIRITUAL AWAKENING,
WE BECAME READY TO MAKE AMENDS
FOR OUR EGO-DOMINATED BEHAVIOR.
MADE A LIST OF ALL PERSONS WE HAD HARMED,
AND BECAME WILLING
TO MAKE AMENDS TO THEM ALL.

Forget it ego!
He's going to attack! Defend yourself!
Who's he kidding? People don't really change! Prepare to fire a round and see if he responds!

Now we take our list and make it real in the world.

We know we are

carrying out this step

with sincerity

when we experience love

for those on our list

(no matter what response

we receive from them).

STEP NINE:
MADE DIRECT AMENDS TO SUCH PEOPLE
WHENEVER POSSIBLE, EXCEPT WHEN TO DO SO
WOULD INJURE THEM OR OTHERS.

Believing, thinking,
talking about:
   God
   Love
   Truth

Experiencing
   God
   Love
   Truth

The first seven steps could actually take place

in a matter of minutes,

or over a much longer period of time.

The point is that the experience

is equally valid.

What is extremely important to realize

is that the experience of God's presence

IS NOT A ONE-TIME EVENT.

It is merely the *first taste* of awakening

from the amnesiac dream.

Be assured that the dream will reassert itself.

The ego dream's favorite way

of lulling its host back to sleep

is to take the experience of God

and make a surviving belief system out of it.

The next two steps are devoted

to recreating the experience of God

in our daily lives.

STEP TEN:

CONTINUED TO TAKE PERSONAL INVENTORY

AND WHEN WE WERE WRONG

PROMPTLY ADMITTED IT.

I think I'll give it a miss today!
I think I'll give it a miss today!
Prayer and meditation Room
To turn our backs on the experience of God is insane.
The source of this insanity is of course ego-idendity (trying to survive).
Because we know that the experience of God is available, listening to ego must cease.

Beware the pitfalls of

   intellectualism and belief.

Just as the experience of love

   should not necessarily lead to

      sex or marriage,

so the experience of God

   should not necessarily lead to

      adherence to any particular religious doctrine.

Also beware ego's advice that you can "do it on your own."

   The support of, and accountability to, others is helpful:

      consider forming a Humans Anonymous support group.

Our entire focus should be on spending

   more and more time in the experience of God—

      in the awakened state.

Loving ourselves and others

   is the only proof we have

      that we are waking up.

STEP ELEVEN:

SOUGHT THROUGH PRAYER AND MEDITATION

TO IMPROVE OUR CONSCIOUS CONTACT

WITH GOD AS WE UNDERSTOOD GOD,

PRAYING ONLY FOR GOD'S WILL FOR US

AND THE POWER TO CARRY THAT OUT.

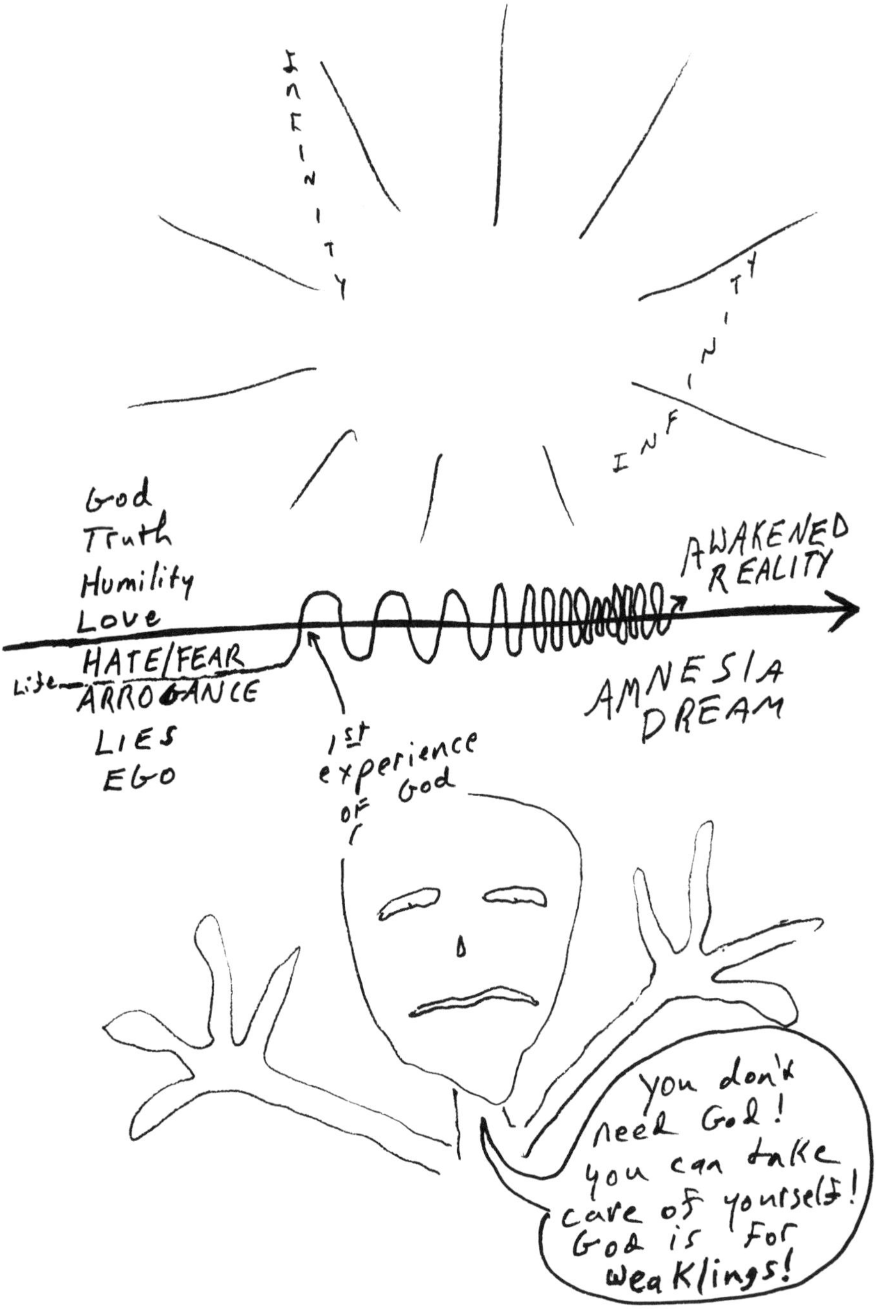
INFINITY
INFINITY
God
Truth
Humility
Love
HATE/FEAR
Life
ARROGANCE
LIES
EGO
AWAKENED REALITY
AMNESIA
DREAM
1st experience of God
You don't need God! You can take care of yourself! God is for weaklings!

This last step means living in love.

If we are not living in the experience of love,

    we are not living in the experience of God,

    we are living under the domination of our ego.

It is just that simple.

The responsibility which accompanies our awakening is two-fold:

    1. to share our awakening with those who still slumber in their pain, and

    2. to never delude ourselves that we are in any way superior to them.

STEP TWELVE:

HAVING HAD A SPIRITUAL AWAKENING

AS THE RESULT OF THESE STEPS,

WE TRIED TO CARRY THIS MESSAGE

TO EGO-DOMINATED HUMAN BEINGS,

AND TO PRACTICE THESE PRINCIPLES

IN ALL OUR AFFAIRS.

12

THE AWAKENING

The spotted hawk swoops by and accuses me, he
    complains of my gab and my loitering.
I too am not a bit tamed, I too am untranslatable,
I sound my barbaric yawp over the roofs of the world.
    The last scud of day holds back for me,
It flings my likeness after the rest and true as any on
    the shadow'd wilds,
It coaxes me to the vapour and the dusk.
    I depart as air, I shake my white locks at the runaway sun,
I effuse my flesh in eddies, and drift it in lacy jags.
    I bequeath myself to the dirt to grow from the flowers I love,
If you want me again look for me under your boot-soles.
    You will hardly know who I am or what I mean,
But I shall be good health to you nevertheless,
And filter and fibre your blood.
    Failing to fetch me at first keep encouraged,
Missing me one place search another,
I stop somewhere waiting for you.

—Walt Whitman, Song of Myself

In the vision there is a room divided in half by a curtain of fire. God is on the other side of the curtain saying "come to me." I know beyond doubt that I will make it through the fire and be with God, but somehow I am afraid and holding back. Looking down, I see my arms are clutching idols, things of myself and the world that I am still attached to — things that are highly combustible and will not survive the flames!

We have looked at how to renounce ego-domination.

Now let us address the question: *what would life*

look like without ego-domination?

First, an overview.

The key to escaping ego-domination is very simple:

tell the truth to the point of experiencing

humility again and again. The idea is to

increasingly identify with experience, and

decreasingly identify with surviving form.

However, attaining humility consistently

happens to be the most difficult task in

all of human life.

This is due to ego's ferocious resistance

to the truth that is bound to expose and destroy it.

The present stage of the Game of God is as difficult as

all other stages of evolution—

the level of difficulty is God-class.

After all, God has spent eighteen billion years or so

evolving to the point of "discovering" His-Her-Its

own existence, so why hurry things now?

God is not about to "wake up" overnight.

God fully intends to savor every step

of the awakening process.

I've found God! This is it!! all my troubles are over!
oh yeah?
NASA space probe
U.S.A.
NASA

We are at that stage of the Game
where the relinquishing of enough ego
to make the initial contact with God is the
next significant step
    in evolution,
      in awakening from amnesia, and
      in the return to God-consciousness.

Escaping ego-domination,
or detaching our identity from ego,
is a **process,** like it or not.
Therefore, to imagine that a fully awakened
merging with God-consciousness is
"just around the evolutionary corner,"
is both false and self-defeating.

One of the weapons the ego will use
to defeat the process of awakening
and regain dominance
is **false expectations of**
"instant and permanent enlightenment."
This false hope will soon discourage and erode
the newfound relationship with God.

What God wants to savor

after so much time spent

in the intolerant and negative

"cage" of form-identity

is the increasing experience

of the beauty and perfection

of life

J U S T   A S   I T   I S.

Remember that the first two purposes of the Game

are for the unlimited to experience the limited

and vice versa.

One or the other of these purposes

is always being brilliantly realized

in our consciousness

(and everywhere else in the universe).

It is important to realize

that while awakening is inevitable,

God has "all the time in the universe"...

time means nothing to the eternal.

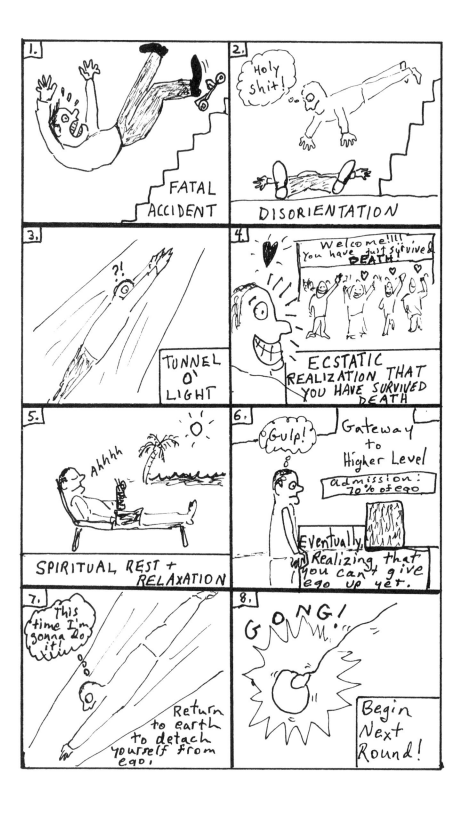

The question will arise, *"What happens when we die?"*

The answer is, no one knows. However, in the context of the universe as a Game, with God as the underlying truth, we may draw some logical conclusions.

Death, as oblivion and/or nothing, does not exist. God is *everything*, so there is no such thing as "nothing."

Death is a deliberate illusion to make life interesting and exciting. We are not separate, nor is anything else, from God. There is only God, awakening from self-induced amnesia, and "death" is a necessary part of the Game.

Our theory of what happens after death is based upon reincarnation. People who have reported near-death experiences clearly have a strong sense of self-identity after leaving their physical bodies. This would seem to indicate that ego survives death. What ego "adheres to" is the underlying spirit of God (still in form-identity amnesia). The ego shell which encapsulates spirit is what has been called the "soul." The extent to which we die attached to our egos determines our ability to advance to a higher level of play. Recall the wall of fire cartoon on page 292. Our inability to pass such a barrier will require us to return to earth and lose more of our "idols"—our false god of ego.

Reuniting with God is assured because GOD IS ALL.

Love truth God

GOD
EGO
Human Love   First experience of God   wow!   PROCESS

TIME

The Sea of Flight Fight Form-Survival Behavior

Amnesia is like a dream. The degree to which the dreamer awakens to the reality of the awakened state depends ENTIRELY upon the dreamer's willingness to abandon the false reality of the dream.

Let us say that the ocean represents the amnesiac state of God-as-form, a sea of flight/fight form-survival behavior, and let us say that the air and dry ground above sea level represent the awakened state of God-consciousness. Let us further imagine ourselves to be fish, trapped in the watery depths of survival behavior.

The closest most of us come to experiencing God's presence (usually without realizing it) is when we love. *When we experience love we are like those fish who briefly sip the air at the surface of the ocean and then return to the deep.*

Those who surrender in humility to God are like the fish who leap momentarily into the air—they become aware of a new and awakened context (and of the watery "cage" they have just escaped).

The light and air of God are meant to become habit-forming and to draw us from dark unconsciousness towards the light of truth. We are to be like the first creature who renounced the sea for dry land.

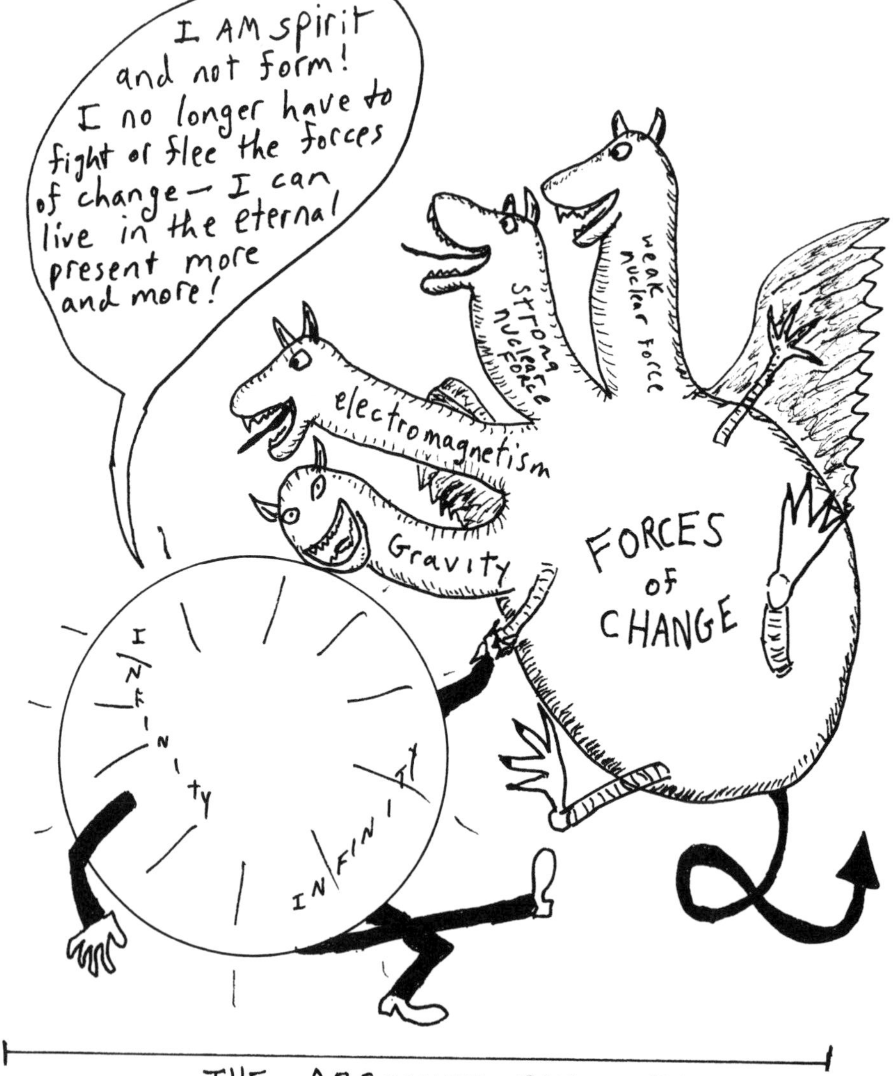

THE ABSOLUTE PRESENT
(NO TIME)

The process of transcendence involves the systematic renunciation of the dreaming state of ego for the awakened state of God. The time spent in the experience of God's presence, an event, is the only time we are (comparatively) free of ego-domination. It is only within this experience that we can answer the question *"what does life without ego look like?"*

Egoless life looks, first and foremost, like love: *the experience of unconditional acceptance of what is*. Experience leaves the intellect behind and brings us closer to the absolute present (thinking takes time and attention so our awareness is always lagging behind reality). This is the meaning of **Be Here Now**.

Being in the experience of God is the only place where we leave off our painful and exhausting survival behavior and experience **satisfaction, peace, joy, inspiration, creative insight, rest, and love without condition**.

The reason we experience these divine states is because suddenly we are no longer *surviving as form* and no longer *perceiving existence as a threat*. Only in the experience of God do we experience relief.

HERE IS THE STATE OF REST THAT
EVOLUTION HAS ALWAYS SOUGHT.

Time →

Faith Faith Faith

Faith Faith Faith Faith

Faith Fa

FIRST Experience

second Experience

THIRD Experience

Life is *forever changed*

by a single experience

of the reality of God.

Even if we never experience God again,

we can never deny

that God is real.

Anyone who has ever been in love

has no doubt about having once loved—

the experience of God

is just that undeniable

(indeed it is the *same experience*).

Once we experience God

we must rely on faith

to carry us through the times

when ego reasserts its control.

We define faith as:

a conviction which is based upon

experiential and empirical evidence.

Faith is the bridge

that must carry us

from God experience to God experience.

The more we open ourselves to the experience of
   God (*Step Eleven*) the more our lives
   will be transformed.
We can easily measure the extent of our
   transformation (our relationship with God)
   by our behavior.
Life without ego looks:

   compassionate, forgiving,

   understanding, caring,

   generous, considerate,

   kind, encouraging,

   supportive, helpful,

   patient, selfless,

   honest...**loving**, in a word.

There is either the dream of ego
   or the awakened truth of God.
When ego is present there is fear and hate,
   usually pretending to be "good."
When God is present, there is only love.

If we are willing to look and tell the truth,
   there is no confusion about whether God or ego
   is in control.

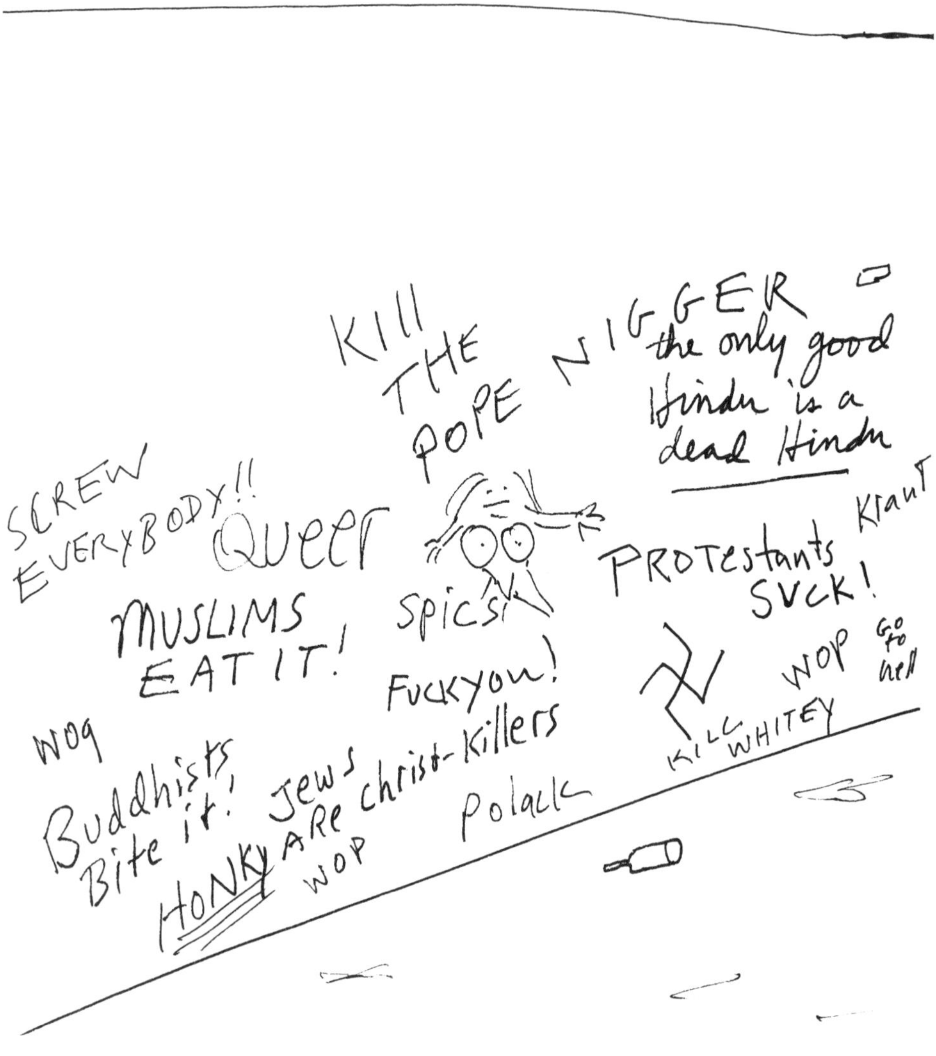
KILL THE POPE
NIGGER
the only good Hindu is a dead Hindu
SCREW EVERYBODY!!
Queer
Kraut
PROTEstants SUCK!
MUSLIMS EAT IT!
Spics!
Fuck you!
wog
WOP
Go to hell
KILL WHITEY
Buddhists Bite it!
Jews ARE christ-killers
Polack
HONKY
WOP

If humans began
to take God seriously, and
abandoned their ego-corrupted religions
(the ones which allow them
to "believe" in God
and still retain their egos)
then human society would
quickly begin to change
in a beautiful and profound way.

In fact, relationship with God
is the only thing that will save us
from the supreme agony of ego-enslavement:
ego-domination will
ultimately lead
to human self-extinction.

Don't stand too close to that long-haired wierdo, he probably has lice! What a bum! Does he realize what he looks like?
Check out the Organization man in the monkey suit! Chained to a briefcase and probably never had an original thought in his life! Does he realize what he looks like?
Robot #1
Robot #2

Many people think that
  if they renounced their ego-identity it would mean that
they would lose their "*individuality*" and
  become "*robots*" with no "*freedom*" whatsoever.
Such dismal automatons would be
  hopeless, dangerous, bland, and dull.
In fact, they would look exactly like human beings!

We have talked at length about
  what being trapped in ego looks like.
It looks like fear, hate, loneliness, and pain.
  The talk of "*losing one's individuality*"
is simply another trick on the part of the parasitic
  ego to keep its host stuck with it forever.
Ego-identity is the true robot state:
  blind and endless obedience
to the dictates of an absolute tyrant.
  Under ego-domination,
we are stimulus-response machines,
  with rigid preconceptions which prevent
any true spontaneity or freedom.
  True freedom and individuality are the rewards for
following the path of ego renunciation.
  In God alone is freedom and the way out.

INFINITY

LOVE

INFINITY

The absolute acceptance of absolute Reality:
THE EXPERIENCE OF BEING

With the overthrow of ego-domination, human society would begin to function optimally.

Love (unconditional God love as opposed to human love) *always produces appropriate behavior.* Love is sanity.

Human beings would begin to help each other
from the best of motivations:

not because the law demanded it of them,

not because their consciences goaded them into

doing the "right thing,"

but simply because **love feels better than anything else on Earth**. We naturally want to do good things for those we love.

Even those who do not believe in God could only want to spend as much time in the state of unconditional love as possible. Love is the finest experience available to us.

Unconditional God love is the only solution to all of our problems, both social and personal, because unconditional God love is the awakened state of God and the way to win the Game.

∞

Universe Director

Universe Sub-Director

Super Group Supervisor

Galactic Manager

Sector Manager

HUMAN

ANT

Cell

ATOM

BIG BANG

∞

SIMULTANEOUS
LEVELS
OF
GOD-CONSCIOUSNESS

Ultimately, God is the only truth; the supreme reality. God created the universe for the experience of limitation, which includes relationship—innumerable variations of *things relating to things.*

So far, we have related to one another almost entirely from flight/fight survival behavior.

The Third Law of the Universe—

>*transcend survival as form—*

>>does not say "*stop existing,*"

>>nor does it say "*stop surviving.*"

What it **does** say is *stop identifying with surviving form,*

>*and instead identify with God, Who is eternal spirit,*

>*Who is infinite awareness, Who is All.*

This opens the way to **loving** relationships on all levels: with ourselves, with other humans, with our planet, with our universe, and with God (Who is all of the above).

We will, ultimately, lose ALL form identity and merge with God. In the meantime, there is much fun to be had in increasingly awakened relationships...to the point of consciously realizing the **Third Purpose of the Universe**:

>*For the Unlimited To Experience The Unlimited.*

In the process of losing and regaining God-identity,

>**God is able to re-experience**

>**and fully "appreciate" Godself.**

The Third Purpose is realized

in the Reunification of Humpty:

all sense of separation from God disappears

and there is only God.

We are not "separate creatures" who are "victims" of existence, we are expressions of God experiencing limitation and overcoming it. **We are God in disguise.** "We" are not God: God is *everything* and "we" are, ultimately, illusion. Our destiny lies in the realm of the infinite—the unlimited. It is only through experiencing the truth

GOD IS ALL

that we can forgive God...to the extent of realizing that *no forgiveness is, or ever has been, necessary.* God is, after all, only "doing this" to Godself. Only when this realization is experientially attained are we able to love God.

This experience of *God Is All* is attained through implementing the Third Law of the universe: transcending survival as form, that is, *renouncing ego-domination for the experience of God.*

Transcending survival as form is the only way to achieve

LASTING PEACE, TRUTH, LOVE, AND SATISFACTION,

and is the only way

TO WIN THE GAME OF GOD.

GLOSSARY

BELIEF a conviction which is not necessarily based upon any empirical or experiential evidence; a non-physical surviving thought-form.

COMPASSION the perception, arising from the experience of love, that all survival behavior proceeds from a form of insanity, and thus is entirely forgivable.

EGO-IDENTITY the primary survival identity of a human being; a non-physical surviving form comprised of surviving prevailing beliefs; an awareness of self as distinct from the physical body; SYN personality.

ENLIGHTENMENT the experience which occurs in proportion to a human being's realization of the extent of his or her ignorance, mortality, helplessness, and pride.

EVIL believing in, and/or acting on, a false belief. A belief is false to the extent to which it fails to admit to its limitations: the only limitations are those imposed by ignorance of the absolute truth. SYN sin.

EXPERIENCE being, free of a survival identity. SYN God, love, truth.

FAITH a conviction which is based upon experiential and empirical evidence; a non-physical surviving thought-form.

FEAR in volitional forms, the attempt to escape a perceived threat to structural integrity; the *flight* half of flight/fight survival behavior.

FORM any observable entity; a thing apparently separate and distinct from everything else by virtue of its being surrounded by *not-that-thing*.

GOD Being, free of a survival identity; the absolute awareness of absolute reality; SYN. truth, love, and experience.

HATRED in volitional forms, the attempt to overpower, harm, or destroy a perceived threat to structural integrity; the aggressive, or *fight* half, of flight/fight survival behavior.

HUMILITY the experience which occurs in proportion to a human being's realization of the extent of his or her ignorance, mortality, helplessness, and pride.

LAWS OF THE UNIVERSE 1. exist as form 2. survive as form 3. transcend survival as form.

LOVE the experience of unconditional acceptance of what is.

MIND a memory bank comprised of stored sensory input data, pro-survival fact data, and prevailing belief data.

NON-PHYSICAL FORM a specific mind-generated entity: a thought, belief system, concept, etc., produced by, and stored in, the mind.

NON-VOLITIONAL FORM any physical entity which is incapable of reacting to its environment; any thing which is passively manipulated by the interactional forces; inorganic; non-living.

PERSONALITY individual identity as expressed in behavior and attitudes.

PREVAILING BELIEF a belief which cannot be consistently verified as true within the physical environment; e.g. *walking under a ladder brings bad luck.*

PRIMARY SURVIVAL IDENTITY the essential structure of a form, physical or non-physical, which dictates its survival behavior.

PRO-SURVIVAL FACT a belief which can be consistently verified as true in the physical environment; e.g. *fire is hot.*

PURPOSES OF THE UNIVERSE 1. for the unlimited to experience limitation. 2. for the limited to experience the unlimited. 3. for the unlimited to experience the unlimited.

SURVIVAL the effort of a specific form to maintain its existent structural integrity; a form's resistance to change.

TRANSCEND SURVIVAL AS FORM a process of willful detachment from form; ceasing to identify with form.

TRUTH the absolute awareness and absolute acceptance of absolute reality [see God, love, experience].

VOLITIONAL FORM any entity (physical or non-physical) which is capable of reacting to its environment, from single cell to ego-identity.

CREDITS FOR QUOTES

Opening page, Chapter Ten, Chapter Twelve from *Leaves Of Grass*, by Walt Whitman, Random House Modern Library edition.

Introduction page, *Catch-22*, Joseph Heller, Dell Publishing Company.

Part One, Albert Einstein quotes from *Coming of Age In the Milky Way*, Timothy Ferris, William Morrow and Company.

Chapter One, Chapter Ten, Lao Tsu, *Tao te Ching*, translation by Gia-Fu Feng and Jane English, Vintage Books, a division of Random House.

Chapter Two/Chaung-Tzu; Chapter Six/Aristotle; Chapter Four/Sir Julian Huxley, Nietzsche; Chapter Nine/Buddha; Chapter Ten/Analects of Confucius, from *Philosophy An Introduction To The Art Of Wondering*, by James L. Christian, Holt, Rinehart and Winston.

Part Two, Part Three, Chapter Eleven, *The Bible*, New International Translation.

Chapter Three, Percy Byssyhe Shelly, *Prometheus Unbound*; Isaac Newton, the *Principia*.

Chapter Five/Jane Goodall; Chapter Six/Arthur C. Clarke; *Living Philosophies*, edited by Clifton Fadiman, Doubleday.

Chapter Seven, Tom Robbins, *Another Roadside Attraction*, Doubleday; Douglas Adams, *The Restaurant at the end of the Universe*, Pocket Books, a division of Simon and Schuster.

Chapter Eight, Chapter Eleven, *Bhagavad Gita*, translated by Juan Mascaro, Penguin Books.

Chapter Eight, Thomas Wolfe, *Look Homeward, Angel*, Charles Scribner's Sons; John Kennedy Toole, *A Confederacy of Dunces*, Grove Press.

Chapter Nine, Sioux Indian quote from *The Family of Man*, published for the Museum of Modern Art by Simon and Schuster; Anne Frank, *The Diary of Anne Frank*, Washington Square Press, Pocket Books, a division of Simon and Schuster.

Chapter Eleven, *Alcoholics Anonymous*, the Big Book, Alcoholics Anonymous World Services Inc.

Definition of "ego" and "transcend" from *Webster's New World Dictionary*, Second College Edition.

Beans Taste Fine, the song quoted in Chapter Two, by Shel Silverstein, Hollis Music, Inc., BMI.

ALCOHOLICS ANONYMOUS DISCLAIMER

We wish to thank Alcoholics Anonymous for the use of the 12 steps. Here are the 12 steps in their original form:

1. We admitted we were powerless over alcohol—that our lives had become unmanageable.
2. Came to believe that a Power greater than ourselves could restore us to sanity.
3. Made a decision to turn our will and our lives over to the care of God *as we understood Him.*
4. Made a searching and fearless moral inventory of ourselves.
5. Admitted to God, to ourselves, and to another human being the exact nature of our wrongs.
6. Were entirely ready to have God remove all these defects of character.
7. Humbly asked Him to remove our shortcomings.
8. Made a list of all persons we had harmed, and became willing to make amends to them all.
9. Made direct amends to such people wherever possible, except when to do so would injure them or others.
10. Continued to take personal inventory and when we were wrong promptly admitted it.
11. Sought through prayer and meditation to improve our conscious contact with God *as we understood Him,* praying only for knowledge of His will for us and the power to carry that out.
12. Having had a spiritual awakening as the result of these steps, we tried to carry this message to alcoholics, and to practice these principles in all our affairs.

The twelve steps are reprinted with permission of Alcoholics Anonymous World Services Inc. Permission to reprint and adapt this material does not mean that A.A. has reviewed or approved the contents of this publication nor that A.A. agrees with the views expressed herein. A.A. is a program of recovery from alcoholism—use of the steps in connection with programs and activities which are patterned after A.A., but which address other problems, does not imply otherwise.

ORDER FORM

Please send me _____ copies of The Game of God.

I have enclosed a check or money order for $12.95 plus $2.00 shipping for each book ordered. (Quantity discounts are available.)

Name_____

Address_____

City_____State_____Zip_____

Please allow 4-6 weeks for delivery.

Humans Anonymous Press

P.O. Box 170045

St. Louis MO 63117